In My
Father's Country

In My
Father's Country

A Nigerian Journey

Adewale Maja-Pearce

HEINEMANN : LONDON

William Heinemann Ltd
10 Upper Grosvenor Street, London W1X 9PA
LONDON   MELBOURNE
JOHANNESBURG   AUCKLAND

First published 1987
© Adewale Maja-Pearce 1987
ISBN 0 434 44170 8

Printed and bound in Great Britain by
Billing & Son Ltd, Worcester

To the memory of my father,
Dr Jameson Akintola Pearce
(1914–1981)

Acknowledgment

The author and publisher acknowledge with thanks Penguin
Books for the use of the Clapperton journal extracted from
African Discovery, M. Perham and J. Simmons (eds), 1948.

Today I write this fiction for my father,
who was right. Truth *is*
the only thing worth searching for,
though histories be proved untrue
and travelogues distortions.
        (from 'Truth' by Stewart Brown)

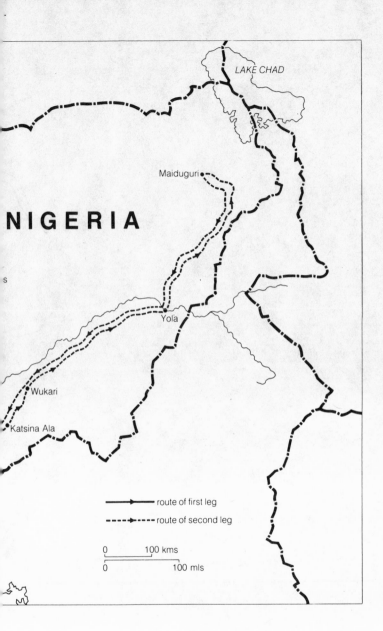

LAKE CHAD

Maiduguri

NIGERIA

Yola

Wukari

Katsina Ala

route of first leg
route of second leg

0   100 kms
0   100 mls

I

'Hassle, hassle, hassle; too much hassle.' Her accent was an odd mixture of Nigerian and cockney. She was short, round, light-skinned; late thirties. She said she had been living in London for the last fifteen years. She went back to Nigeria as often as she could, which wasn't as often as she would have liked. Her father, an old man now, was looked after by another of his daughters. She herself couldn't think of living in Nigeria. Life there was too difficult.

A relative of hers was getting married. She had baked a cake. It was in one of the many cardboard boxes piled up around her in the departure lounge as we waited for our call. She had fallen into conversation with me only because I was travelling light. She had already enlisted the help of another man. Now the three of us made fitful conversation in the manner of travellers brought together by accident and soon to part forever – who had last been back, when, for how long.

I had last been back two years before, after a long absence. I had only stayed three weeks. It was shortly after my father had died; and it says something about my relationship with him when he had been alive that it was only his death which had made my return possible. It had been because of him that I had first left when I was sixteen.

I was travelling by Sierra Leone Airlines. It was a new

airline. Nobody had ever heard of it before. They had only the one plane, a battered Boeing 707 piloted by a Jordanian. Although it was cheap it wasn't by any means the cheapest. Balkan Air had that distinction. I had travelled with Balkan Air on my previous trip. The journey had taken sixteen hours altogether. That included a six-hour stop-over in Sofia. Sofia airport is a dump.

I hadn't intended to travel via Freetown. My agent in Tunbridge Wells (Mr Woodward, Best East-West, Specialists in Africa) had found an inexpensive flight on Egypt Air. The Egypt Air flight stopped overnight in Cairo. I loved the idea of Cairo. Even the name is magic. Alan Ross of *London Magazine*, who was ultimately responsible for this trip and who I had seen just before I had left, called it 'a dirty little hole on the edge of the desert'. That didn't make me change my mind. In the event I never saw Cairo. The booking clerk at the Air Egypt office had made a mistake. When I arrived at Heathrow, in what I thought was good time, I discovered that the plane had left three hours before. The litter at the check-in counter told me as much even as the woman at the British Airways Information Desk lingered over the time-table and searched for the comforting words. In the end she could only doubtfully suggest that I phone the head office, but since it was gone five we both knew it was probably futile. I phoned Mr Woodward instead. The poor man was mortified, though he wasn't to blame. He went straight into action. An hour and several whiskies later I was booked on the Sierra Leone Airways flight for the following day. He had managed to arrange this through a contact of his; he even came to the airport to make sure that I got on the flight. Cairo would have to wait.

We finally left London at midnight, an hour behind schedule. We picked up a consignment of noisy German holidaymakers at Las Palmas and arrived in Freetown at seven in the morning. The airport at Freetown was a shabby affair of dilapidated buildings and servile officials. The policeman who showed us the way to the transit lounge – a grand name for a concrete hut with uncomfortable seats and an empty bar – hung around for the tip no one had any intention of giving him. We turned our backs on him and went in search of amusement, and he trudged off into the fine tropical drizzle that had greeted us as we had stepped on to the tarmac. It was the kind of servility that one associated with colonialism. The only difference was that most of the travellers were Nigerians. I knew very well that the officials at Lagos might also attempt to part you from your money, but there is all the difference in the world in the manner in which they will do so: with contempt.

It was in Freetown that the woman I was helping told me I had too much Nigerian currency. Forty naira was twice what the authorities permitted anyone to bring into the country. I was nervous enough as it was. Foolishly, my first thought was to throw away the excess. Then I caught sight of a stall. It was filled with the usual paraphernalia: wood carvings, bits of jewellery, native dresses. The stall-holder was reluctant to sell me a shirt for twenty naira. He preferred sterling or dollars. In the end I convinced him that since I was paying well over the odds he couldn't really lose.

We finally made Lagos at three in the afternoon. By now I was in a state of nervous exhaustion. My hand was shaking as I filled out the disembarkation card. I had good reason. The officials at Lagos are notorious. Nigerians generally have a terrible reputation abroad. They are considered arrogant, aggressive and loud, and so they are. It is a source of some pride to them. To get a taste of the country one only has to try and get a visa at the High Commission in London, otherwise known as the Nigeria High Confusion. Not one of the officials will be doing what approximates to work. The woman behind the counter will look at you with distaste and throw a form in your direction. She has better things to do.

I needn't have worried. Even before I reached Immigration Control there was a soldier holding up a piece of cardboard with my name scrawled in capital letters. Beside him was a shabbily dressed middle-aged man with a missing front tooth who turned out to be the driver. An officer had sent them to pick me up. The driver took my bag, the soldier took my documents, and we went to the head of every queue. We didn't bother with currency control. I was a guest of the army. In a military state that meant I was a VIP.

I had yet to meet the officer. Six months before, I had met a Nigerian at a seminar on African literature in London. We fell to talking and discovered that we not only shared the same surname but had been at the same boarding school – St Gregory's College, or Gregs for short – in Lagos in the late 1960s. It was an expensive mission school run by the Catholic Church and staffed by Irish priests. He even claimed to remember me, a skinny boy in shorts. Two or three weeks later he phoned me up and announced that he had done some research and discovered we were cousins, as he had suspected. That was fine by me. If he wanted a cousin in England I was happy to oblige. A month before my trip he suggested we do a currency deal. I was to give him £400; a friend in Lagos would give me N1,500. That was four times the official exchange rate. I wasn't complaining.

'Remi said I should give you this,' the soldier said. We were driving towards the city. '200. He didn't know if you would have any naira with you.' It was thoughtful of him and I was touched. I broke open my carton of duty-free cigarettes and offered them a packet each. They didn't smoke.

'Well, what do you think?' the soldier asked and made a movement with his hand at the scene outside.

'I'm impressed,' I said truthfully. I had read about the War

4

Against Indiscipline (WAI), introduced by the army soon after they had overthrown the civilian administration – only the second in the country's twenty-five years – of the flamboyant President Shehu Shagari twenty months before. The country was presently in the middle of the fifth phase, 'Environmental Sanitation'. The other phases had been: Queue Culture (March 1984); Works and Ethics (May 1984); Nationalism and Patriotism (August 1984); Corruption and Economic Sabotage (June 1985). The titles give a good indication of the state the country had been in. On my previous visit I had been shocked and distressed by the filth and squalor of Africa's biggest city.

Nobody knows the exact population of Lagos. Estimates vary between four and seven million. In many ways it is one of the most inconvenient capital cities in the world. This is partly the result of its geography. Lagos proper – the commercial heart of the city – is an island no more than seven square kilometres in area. Most people live on the mainland, which is joined to the island by a series of impressive flyovers. But even these are not enough to solve the traffic congestion during the morning and evening rush-hours. One attempted solution, still in force, was to alternate cars according to whether the last digit on the number plate was an odd or an even number. Those who could afford it simply bought a second car. At any rate it doesn't seem to have made much difference to the volume of traffic.

Lagos is also one of the most dangerous cities in the world. There are some areas of the city where even the most hardened Lagosian wouldn't dare to enter on foot. There is a story of a French camera crew who tried to film in one of the more notorious of these slums, Ajegunle, and got beaten up by the inhabitants before they even had time to set up their equipment. Hardly a day passes but one hears, or reads about, armed robberies and contract killings. It isn't unusual for the armed robbers to strike on a busy road. Even getting into a taxi in the middle of the day is a hazardous enterprise. I met someone who had been taken by the driver and his companion to another slum, dragged inside a building and beaten senseless, all for the sake of a wristwatch and some spare change. One only has to see the poverty to realize why. I happened to go to Ajegunle once in the company of a sailor. He was visiting a family of five who lived in one room. This room, which was no more than ten square feet, was below the level of the road and faced an open gutter. At the height of the rainy season it would be flooded. Their only consolation, if one could call it a consolation, was that they had nothing to fear from the armed robbers.

Those who have money, and therefore everything to fear, turn their houses into fortresses. They lock themselves in at night behind steel doors and rarely emerge until morning. One sometimes wonders whether the rewards of living in such a dangerous city can be worth the constant worry that your turn may be next, that you may be awakened in the darkness to hear your wall caving in as fifteen or twenty men, armed to the teeth, launch an assault that will almost certainly spell your end. At such a time phoning the police will be a waste of time. The chances are that the phone won't work; and if it does work, that the sergeant on duty will take down your name and address, tell you to hold on, and do absolutely nothing: why should he get himself killed protecting something that doesn't belong to him?

To think in terms of your friendly neighbourhood policeman is to make a terrible mistake. Consider the following story. Two neighbours were having an argument. Things got out of hand and a window was smashed. Somebody called the police. They turned up half-an-hour later, parked the car at the bottom of the road, and sent a child to call the men. When the men appeared they were shoved into the back seat and told to start bidding. One of them reached N200. It was more than the other could match. The first man paid and went; the other was beaten so badly that it was all he could do to crawl back to his house. This story was recounted in a matter-of-fact tone as we sat on a balcony in the late afternoon sipping soft drinks. The man who told us the story shrugged his shoulders and laughed and went on to discuss other matters. 'That's Lagos,' was his only comment.

I was to later witness a scene that will remain with me forever. It was outside one of the department stores in downtown Lagos, about mid-day. The street was packed with people and noisy with the traffic. A man came out of one of the stores and was shouted at by another. Suddenly, from somewhere in the crowd, a policeman appeared brandishing a whip. Without bothering to find out what had happened he set about the man. He was presently joined by three of his colleagues, who also laid into the man. They whipped him until the sweat was pouring down their faces. I remember particularly that one of the policemen, in his haste, slipped and fell. When they finally let up the poor wretch was covered in blood and had to be taken to the hospital. Perhaps they thought he had been shoplifting; perhaps they just felt like flexing their muscles.

And yet, for all that, Lagos is an exciting city. When people say, 'I couldn't think of living anywhere else,' I know what they mean. There is an energy and a vitality about Lagos which challenges the visitor. Everybody is on the make; everybody is hustling twenty-four hours a day. There is no such thing as having too much. A schoolfriend I met soon after my arrival, a doctor with his own clinic, had a profitable little sideline selling ties to our old school, which he bought in bulk on his frequent trips to London. That he was already making money hand over fist was neither here nor there. This energy extends right down to the boys and girls who take advantage of the go-slows to peddle their wares: apples, potatoes, cassette tapes, ironing boards, washing powder, trousers, wrist watches, handkerchiefs. It is perfectly possible to do all your shopping on your way to and from work. The disadvantage of this kind of rampant capitalism is chaos. That is what happened under the civilians. A human corpse could remain in the middle of the street for weeks on end since it didn't pay anybody to take it away. Hence the War Against Indiscipline.

Now, as we drove towards the city, I noticed that the great mounds of garbage had been cleared, the open gutters had been cleaned and all the public buildings had been given a coat of whitewash. So-called 'illegal structures' – rickety additions to existing houses often serving as makeshift shops – had been pulled down; there were few hawkers about; everywhere people queued. To see people queuing for a bus in Lagos is an extraordinary sight to those who know the city.

'You understand, we Nigerians have to learn the hard way. Without the guiding wisdom of our leader we can't even keep our surroundings clean,' the soldier said.

'Yes, that's right,' the driver nodded vigorously. He would have nodded vigorously to anything. I doubt he cared one way or the other as long as he kept his job.

'You saw how it was under the civilians? Everybody stealing, no discipline,' he added.

Presently we arrived at Remi's house. He lived in the old area of Yaba. The houses here, dating from the nineteenth century, were built by emancipated slaves from Brazil who, tracing their ancestry back to the West Coast of Africa, settled in Lagos and became wealthy traders, notably in slaves. Lagos was one of the chief ports for the export of slaves until it was finally turned into a colony by the British in 1861. Many of these houses have since fallen into decay. There is a melancholy about them which speaks of an age that has long since passed. It is only the names that are left:

Cardoso, Fernandez, Marinho, Vincent, Da Costa and Da Silva are among the prominent Lagos families.

A boy came to collect my bags. I thanked the soldier and offered him a N20 note. He shook his head: 'Thank you, no. You can give it to the driver if you like.' I couldn't tell if I had offended him, but if he was the spirit of the new regime then things were hopeful. The driver had less qualms. The money disappeared into his pocket before I had even offered it to him.

I was taken into the sitting room. A young man came to greet me and offered me a drink. My bags were taken to another room. He switched on the air-conditioner and asked me what I would like to eat. I wasn't hungry. I hadn't slept in twenty-four hours and my nerves were ragged. I chain-smoked instead.

The idea of writing a book on Nigeria had occurred to me shortly after my first trip. I had calculated I would need £2,000. That would include the return airfare and enough to leave behind for my family. One day, out of the blue, I received a letter from a publisher. Someone had sent him a photocopy of the 4000-word essay I had written on that trip and which had appeared in *London Magazine*. He had liked it. He invited me to lunch and asked me what my plans were.

'I'm going to write a travel book on Nigeria,' I said.

'When?'

'As soon as somebody pays me.'

'Tell me about it.'

I started by giving him a few facts about the country: that with almost 100 million people it supports nearly a quarter of Africa's total population; that it is far and away Africa's wealthiest state, with a gross national product nearly half that of the other forty-five black African nations combined; that with an area three times the size of Britain, most of it arable, it could easily feed the entire continent by itself. In short, I told him that Nigeria has the potential to become one of the world's most powerful nations. It is the only country in Africa with that potential. Moreover, with the approaching twenty-fifth anniversary of independence, it seemed to me that a fresh look at the country would be timely. I also pointed out that I was a good person to do such a book because of my dual heritage: my father was Nigerian, my mother is English; I grew up in Nigeria but now live in England. He asked me to send him a proposal giving more details of what I had said. Within weeks I had signed a contract. Now I would have to produce the goods.

Remi's wife came home as I was thinking about all this. After greeting me, she asked me what I wanted to eat. I still wasn't any hungrier but it would have been rude to refuse. Egusi soup was the first thing that came into my head. It was so long since I had eaten Nigerian food with any regularity that I had forgotten the names of most of the dishes. From her point of view it was a bad choice. I had condemned her to the kitchen for the next three hours, but she took it with good grace.

I was still struggling with the meal, enough for three, when Remi finally returned. He was a round man in a tight-fitting uniform. He had a round, shiny face and he smiled a lot. I took to him at once. He asked me what my plans were. I explained that I was going to travel around the country in two stages. The first stage would take me north as far as Kano by way of Ibadan, Ilorin and Kaduna and back down through Jos, Lokoja and Benin: a month in all. I would then spend about a week in Lagos before heading east for the second stage. I would go as far as Calabar before turning north again and heading for Maiduguri via Wukari and Yola and back down again through Enugu and Onitsha. That would take another month. He pulled out a wad of notes: N750. It was half the agreed amount. He asked me if it was okay if I picked up the balance when I returned to

Lagos after the first leg. That suited me. My visa would have run out by then, which was why I was going to have to break the journey. I would need his help to get it extended.

By the time I had struggled through what I could of the meal it was too late to think of getting over to Akin's place. On the phone from London the day before I had promised to get in touch with him by seven. It was now gone nine. I phoned him all the same and arranged for him to pick me up the following morning.

In the morning everyone was outside cleaning the street in front of their houses. This was Environmental Sanitation in action. Remi, resting on a shovel, was busy supervising the rest of his household.

Akin came to collect me. He almost hadn't made it. On the way over he had been stopped by some soldiers on duty who wanted to commandeer his Mini to transport rubbish to the outskirts of the city, until he had pointed out that his car didn't have a boot. As we drove back to his place we passed less fortunate drivers who were having difficulty keeping their tempers in check. Not that they had much choice in the matter. One didn't fool with the army.

Akin and I had been best friends at school. He knew about my family background and my problems with my father. In all the years I had been in England we hadn't communicated. I had seen him again for the first time on my previous visit. The idea that there might still have been something between us had never really occurred to me: I had simply thought it might be amusing to see what had happened to him in the intervening years. But I had underestimated him. It didn't take me long to realize that as far as he was concerned nothing had changed. Where I was casual he was solicitous. He couldn't do enough for me. He ferried me about everywhere; he wouldn't hear of me paying for anything; he was anxious that I approved of his fiancée. In this way he became, unexpectedly, my link with the country, a link I had assumed had been finally broken with my father's death.

Akin was a lawyer. After working for eight years for a relative of his, one of the country's top lawyers, he had branched out on his own. His chambers were an extension of his bungalow in the family compound. Most of the bungalow – two bedrooms, bathroom, dining/living room, kitchen – and all of the chambers he had built himself from what had originally been the servants' quarters. His elder married brother lived in the second bungalow; his mother, sister and junior brother lived in the third. In England your brother is a possibility; in Nigeria he is a fact. I was to learn something about the delicate network of responsibilities that existed in Nigeria between members of the same family. The youngest brother was unemployed, so the other two made sure he had enough pocket money. When Akin's wife wanted to go to the market, it was the youngest brother who drove her. Akin himself was responsible for maintaining the grounds, to which end he employed a gardener; the elder brother took care of the security arrangements. They were a close-knit unit, forever in and out of each other's houses, and there was a genuine sense in which all the children in the compound were the responsibility of all the adults.

Akin employed a junior lawyer and a clerk. Watching him with his clerk, I was to remember, also, something of the base level of brutality that exists in Nigerian society and which I thought I had forgotten.

I was impressed with the plush surroundings and the book-lined walls and said so.

'To be young in this country is a handicap,' he said. 'I have to reassure my clients with all this.' This was true, but it was only half the truth. He himself enjoyed his material comforts both for their own sake and for the way they reflected on him. He tried hard to cultivate the image of the successful Nigerian male. He didn't quite pull it off, partly because he was still, at 33, relatively young, partly because he simply didn't have the right build. He was too slight: he should have had trouble keeping his trousers around his belly, which is a sure sign that you've made it. He buzzed his wife on the intercom.

'Ade is here,' he said. His wife, Shade, came in with some coffee. When I had first met her she had just returned from England with a Master's degree in law. Now a research fellow at the university, she had just given birth to their first child.

She was very dark and very beautiful. Like most Nigerian women she wore traditional dress much of the time. This consisted of a loose blouse with wide sleeves and an ankle-length skirt usually in identical material. The skirt is really just a single piece of cloth wrapped round the waist: it is in the elaborate patterns and the vivid colours – predominantly blues and greens – that make the women such an arresting sight, particularly when the whole is completed with a headtie. These women are seen at their best at the social functions that are a dominant feature of Nigerian social life: naming ceremonies, remembrance parties, christenings, weddings, wake-keepings. Hardly a weekend passed that Akin and Shade did not go off to one of these. The women of the family throwing the party would all be dressed in identical material purchased in bulk and made up by a seamstress, but each one would be distinguished from the others by the individual manner in which she wore her head-tie. Many of these functions took place out of doors. They occupied an entire side-street and the music was provided by as many as three bands in competition with each other. It was at one of these functions that I noticed what looked like a smartly dressed ten-year-old boy being escorted from one table to the next. The boy seemed to be something of a curiosity, and elicited much amusement, but it wasn't until he suddenly turned in my direction that I understood why: he had the wrinkled face of an old man. The juxtaposition of the young body and the old face was unnerving.

I explained my itinerary to Akin. It was typical of him that he immediately arranged to do some business in Ibadan, which was to be my first place of call. I knew almost nothing of the country outside Lagos. As a child I had been to Abeokuta, my father's home-town, perhaps half-a-dozen times. These pilgrimages had been family occasions: as the big doctor from the big city, his presence was highly sought after. What he thought about them I don't know; for both my brothers and I they meant hours of boredom sitting in some distant relative's uncomfortable living room sipping soft drinks until we were sick. My boredom was compounded by my inability to speak Yoruba.

That I never learnt Yoruba is rather curious, but understandable: it was partly having an English mother; it was partly living in Ikoyi, a predominantly European suburb of the city. The primary schools I attended – St Saviour's and Corona – were staffed exclusively by Europeans for the children of expatriates and the few Nigerians who had made it. Those were the days before Independence. On Mayday we danced round the Maypole; once a week I went to a meeting of the cubs. The country became independent when I was seven years old. By then I was a proper little colonial with a faultless English accent.

For many years after I left Nigeria I didn't admit to anyone that I couldn't speak my father's language. It was like a dark, shameful secret which cast doubt on my 'Africanness'. The matter was further complicated by the fact that I was, after all, half English. I even had a British passport: I was born in London, where my father was qualifying to be a surgeon at the time. But in England I was taken to be a foreigner. I was continually being asked where

I was from. I would invariably say Nigeria; but it would have been equally accurate, in some ways more so, if I had said England. That I didn't was telling. By rejecting my Englishness, I was colluding in a subtle form of racism. I couldn't be English, I was assuring them, since I was clearly not white. And yet, by the same token, I wasn't Nigerian either, since I was clearly not black. The other day I came across the following passage in the autobiography of Langston Hughes, *The Big Sea*, in which he describes a journey to the West Coast of Africa in the 1920s:

> But they only laughed at me and shook their heads and said: 'You, white man! You, white man!'
> It was the only place in the world where I've ever been called a white man. They looked at my copper-brown skin and straight black hair – like my grandmother's Indian hair, except a little curly – and they said: 'You, white man'.

There was a popular refrain which children used to chant at my brothers and me, particularly on our visits to Abeokuta:

> *Oyinbo* pepper,
> If you eat pepper
> You go yellow more more.

Oyinbo means white man. I remember an English friend asking me once why, if I was considered black in Europe, I wasn't considered white in Africa. It was entirely logical, and he was right. I lied to him: I didn't want to admit that I was considered different in my father's country.

But the question of colour, which I find too tedious for words, only clouded the real issue. If I was a hybrid of two powerful cultures, my colour was only the outward symbol of a deeper confusion of identity. It was at least partly in an

15

attempt to come to terms with this confusion – I couldn't say quite what I had in mind – that I was undertaking this journey. I didn't expect to come up with any answers. This is only one man's account of a journey through a country to which he is forever tied by blood.

2

IBADAN WAS FOUNDED in the 1830s as a result of the break-up of the old Oyo Empire. By the 1850s it had emerged as the most important Yoruba town, with an estimated population of 65,000. Its power rested on its military superiority which enabled it to control the trade routes between the Europeans on the coast and the Hausa-Fulani Empire in the interior, much as Oyo had done at its height in the seventeenth and eighteenth centuries. A century later, with half-a-million inhabitants, it was the largest city in the country. Although it has since been overtaken by Lagos, it still remains the focus of Yorubaland. But for all that, it is a disappointing city, a sprawling expanse of tightly packed, tin-roofed houses without a recognizable centre.

We called in first on Akin's client, an elderly woman and relative of his. She lived in one of those old colonial houses of big open rooms and wooden shutters, full of light and space. In the corner where I sat there was a glass-fronted bookcase filled with books on Ireland: *Irish Fairy Tales*; *The Wonders of Ireland*; *Discover Ireland*. There was also a book on Trinity College, Dublin. After the steward had served us our drinks she got down to business.

Her brother had recently died without leaving a will. Akin later explained that this was not unusual. Nigerians

17

believe that to sign your will is effectively to sign your death certificate, a view with which I am in complete sympathy. But her brother had married three times. There was no problem with the first wife, who had died without issue. The second had produced three sons; the third, two daughters.

Her brother and his second wife had separated many years before on mutually accepted terms: he had bought her a school, which she still successfully ran, and had given her a lump sum. Needless to say there was no love lost between the two surviving wives. They both wanted their own children to inherit the estate. At the moment it was the third wife who was occupying all three houses the man had built in his lifetime. There was also the question of a brand-new car and a recently completed bungalow.

As far as the dead man's brothers and sisters were concerned, the wives could fend for themselves. They were only anxious that the sons inherit the properties. This of course put wife number two in an unassailable position. The fact that both the daughters of wife number three were married sealed the matter. Wife number three could be reduced to a pauper overnight. This says something about the position of women in Nigerian society. I was to hear of similar cases again and again. Akin had already told me about the woman whose husband had 'sacked' her. She had had to go to her parents-in-law to ask them to beg their son to take her back. When he still refused there was nothing further she could do. Even worse, he was going to court to sue for custody of the children. There was a good chance that he would win, since he was in a better position financially to look after them. And if he was really a bastard he could forbid her from ever seeing her children again.

From *The* (Lagos) *Guardian* (May 4 1985):

I am confused about these women, over women. Over the ages they have been known to bicker over everything and

18

nothing. But not this time. Right now, there is a cold war raging between two women's groups on, of all things, whether there is merit in suggesting a law that would compel a man leaving his wife after 10 years of marriage to sign off a large chunk of his wealth to her.

The National Council of Women Societies (NCWS) is said to be planning to talk the government into making the law which it hopes will clip the wings of men who may be tempted to drop their wives like a rag, usually after a long marriage session. But another organization, the Muslim Sisters Organization (MSO) does not like the idea. (That should gladden the heart of the men folk, wouldn't it? Wait till you hear it all). The MSO says it is not prepared to oppose a section of the Sharia law which allows Muslim men to keep up to four wives. (Now, smile men!). The sisters also argue that if the NCWS suggestion is bought by the government, it would be tantamount to commercialising marriage, and further making it difficult for honest young men and women to get married. (You see what I mean?).

It also says something about the position of women that my father's mother, who traded in cloth along the coast during the first half of the century, educated all her children with the money she earned: it was she who had paid for their training overseas. It would have been inconceivable for her European counterpart at the time to have done the same. I never met her. She died the year before I was born, which is why my younger sister is named Yetunde, which means 'mother has returned'. By all accounts she was a fearsome woman. Her favourite punishment was to rub pepper into a cut she had made with a razor in the palm of the offending child's hand.

Nigerian history is replete with the exploits of remarkable women traders. The most famous of them all was Madam

Tinubu. Tinubu Square in downtown Lagos is named after her. Little is known about her early life except that she was born in the first half of the last century to a poor farmer in Abeokuta. By 1846 she had built up a lucrative trade in salt and tobacco in Lagos and acted as an agent for the Brazilian slave dealers. With her wealth she became a powerful political force with great influence over the then King of Lagos, Akitoye. She temporarily fell from grace when Akitoye was succeeded by his son, Dosunmu, in a palace revolt. Dosunmu, a weak man, was forced to expel Madam Tinubu from Lagos by the British Consul, Campbell, who was in turn under pressure from the Brazilian traders jealous of her dominance. She returned to her native Abeokuta where she quickly established a flourishing trade in gunpowder, bullets and other weapons of war. Her compound became the unofficial headquarters of other disaffected Lagosians who wanted to avenge themselves on the interfering Consul. But before they could move Abeokuta was attacked by its neighbour, Dahomey. It was she who supplied the army with their weapons, and after the victory of Abeokuta she was rewarded with the title of Iyalode or First Lady. She died childless in 1887.

But however many examples one gives of successful women traders, it will still say nothing at all about the position of women in modern Nigeria. On the one hand it is perfectly true that traditionally women could acquire wealth in their own right; on the other hand traditional societies often discriminated heavily against women: amongst the Yorubas, for instance, wives far from inheriting their husband's estate, were themselves inherited by their deceased husband's family. The position of Igbo women in the east was hardly much better. In most parts of the north women have to contend with the precepts of Islam. The argument from tradition is always double-edged.

When Akin's aunt finished her story she called the steward to bring two dusty metal trunks. They were stuffed to bursting with bundles of papers that hadn't been untied in years, the sum total of a man's life. I saw the look of weariness that crossed Akin's features at the prospect of sorting through them. He had only taken on the case because she was a relative; and because she was a relative he wouldn't be paid for his troubles.

As he made a start, the husband came in. He insisted we take some more beer. I fell into conversation with him. It turned out that he was a doctor and that he had studied at Trinity. I asked him whether he had known my father. As with his wife, I had noticed that my name hadn't registered when we had been introduced. At once his interest was aroused, which is what I had intended.

'Pearce? The son of Jameson Pearce? Excuse me one moment,' he said. He was back again in no time. He was carrying an old photograph album, the kind you rarely see any more. He leafed through it and then pointed to a group photo: five young African men, impeccably dressed in three-piece suits, standing in front of an old building somewhere in Europe.

'You recognize him?' he asked, pointing to the man in the middle. 'Yes, that's your father. We were classmates. And that is Akin's father. He was studying law. This was taken in '47, or it might have been '48, I can't remember.'

We left soon after, Akin clutching an armful of papers he had promised to study at leisure in his office. It was because of me that he had managed to get away so quickly, which might have been in his mind when he took me along with him.

I was planning to stay with Gbadebo, a young Nigerian I had met in London a few weeks before, who worked for a small publishing house. The growth of indigenous publishing in Nigeria in the last decade is one of the most hopeful signs for the emergence of a truly indigenous literature. We had even discussed the possibility of my doing this book for him, but in the end he hadn't been able to match the offer I had received from the British publisher. There were no hard feelings. This was business. I was still invited to stay with him. Since I didn't have his home address, I was anxious to catch him at the office. I hadn't been able to give him an exact date when we had parted in London, nor had I been able to get him on the phone the previous day from Lagos. Communications are unreliable in Nigeria at the best of times. This is what makes it an inconvenient country. The postal service is even worse. Whenever Akin wanted to send a letter he had to use a courier, with all the added expense.

My luck was in. I arrived just as Gbadebo was about to close up for the day. This pattern was to repeat itself throughout the first half of my journey. Superstitious by nature, I would have read all manner of omens into a consistent run of bad luck. But I waved goodbye to Akin with some trepidation. I was truly on my own now.

Gbadebo lived with his elderly parents across the road from the university. His father was a retired Methodist minister. It was a day for meeting people who knew members of my family. My grandfather had also been a Methodist minister. Until he and my father had quarrelled, ostensibly over the way he had treated my mother – 'You knew before you married her that English women have different expectations of marriage' – we used to visit him every Sunday afternoon. By then his eyesight was poor, he was hard of hearing, but otherwise he was as fit as could be expected for a man in his eighties. He was looked after by one of his daughters, a trader who sold foodstuffs from the courtyard of the house. These visits always made my father uneasy. He could hardly sit still for any length of time. One day my grandfather said to him, 'You mean you don't believe in God?' This was after my mother had left. By then my father had married again. Word had reached my grandfather that certain practices – native juju medicine – were taking place in our house. That was the last time they spoke; my father didn't even attend his funeral. But I loved my grandfather. He was a kind man of unshakeable principles. One day, some years after he had died, I wrote to the Methodist Missionary Society for any information they could give me about him. They sent me a copy of the obituary notice taken from the Minutes of a Conference in Nigeria:

Revd. Solomon Adewale Pearce, F.R.G.S., M.B.E., J.P.
He was born in Lagos on 20th August, 1878 by Mr. James Aderamaja Pearce and Mrs. Elizabeth Asake Pearce. He had four other brothers, three of whom predeceased him and a sister who had predeceased him also.

He was educated at the Wesleyan Ereko Primary School and the C.M.S. Grammar School, Lagos.

He entered the Printing Department of the Government service in 1895. He later took successful courses in Music and Elementary Hygiene. He had rapid promotions through examinations and was appointed first class clerk in 1908. In 1904 he was married to Miss Mary Adefowoke at Ereko Methodist Church. This marriage was blessed with six children.

He served as a Special Police in the First World War – 1914–1918 after which in 1918, he read theology in the Methodist Boy's High School under the guidance of the late Revd. Moulton Wood. He was admitted into the ministry of the Methodist Church in 1919 and ordained into full ministry in 1924. He served in various circuits including all Lagos Circuits and Ilesha Circuits. He served the church in various other capacities both as clerical and lay until he retired from active ministry in 1945 at Hoare's Memorial Methodist Church, Yaba. As a Supernumerary, he served the nation zealously and had time to travel widely including the United Kingdom.

In appreciation of his many and varied services he was made a Justice of the Peace, Assessor in the Juvenile Court, Lagos, Fellow of the Royal Geographical Society and Member of the British Empire.

He died peacefully on Thursday, 25th April, 1974 at about the age of ninety-six years. He lived long and served much.

Thanks be to God.

One day I would like to write at length about this man who was born before Nigeria became a British colony and died after the country had achieved Independence. To understand his life would be to understand many things about the colonial encounter, a subject much written about but little understood. Gbadebo's father had known him. As a result his attitude towards me, which had been courteous but distant, underwent a subtle change.

Early the following morning I went to the university. I wanted to make use of the library for a book I was editing on the Nigerian poet, Christopher Okigbo. Okigbo had been a student at Ibadan in the 1950s. Although he had died at the age of thirty-five, killed fighting on the Biafran side during the civil war, he is still generally regarded as the leading English-language Nigerian poet. During his time at the university he had contributed to a student magazine, *The Horn*, edited by his friend and fellow-writer, J. P. Clark. I wanted to go through back copies of the magazine. As far as I knew, the university library was the only place they could be found.

Ibadan was founded in 1948 as an affiliated college of London University. It became an independent university in 1952. For many years it was the country's only non-Islamic institution of higher learning. Despite the enormous growth of indigenous universities since Independence, it still retains a high reputation. Many of the first generation of Nigerian writers had studied there. Okigbo and Clark apart, they included Wole Soyinka, Chinua Achebe, John Munonye, Flora Nwapa and V. C. Ike.

My initial impression was disappointing. The place looked a wreck. There were broken windows in the lecture halls, dirty marks on the walls and puddles of stagnant water in many of the buildings. There was also the problem of toilets. This was not unique to the university. It was a problem which was to plague me throughout my journey and eventually resulted in a severe case of constipation. Even though we were still in the rainy season – in many ways the best time to travel since it is also the coolest, with an average temperature of 75°F – there was no running water. All the toilets were blocked with dried shit and soiled newspaper. I did the best I could and then went to the library. It was nine o'clock. I envisaged a full day's work ahead of me. I should have known better. Life is never simple or staightforward in Nigeria, particularly when one is obliged to deal with officials.

Six men stood around the check-in counter, only one of whom could be said to be working. I ignored them and headed towards the periodicals' section. Before I got very far one of them hissed at me. There is nothing unusual in hissing. It is the way people attract each other's attention. But I have always found it disconcerting. It has a way of sounding both rude and menacing.

'What do you want?' he asked. I began to explain but he quickly cut me short.

'Go and wait there,' he ordered, pointing to a corner near

the entrance. Ten minutes passed; fifteen minutes. The men continued chatting and laughing. I knew it would be a mistake to give in to my anger. They were simply doing what all officials do in Nigeria, which is to exploit to the limit whatever powers they possess. It wasn't personal, unless I made it so. Another man drifted in. It transpired that he was the man I was to see. They spoke to him, he glanced at me, and then he went off in another direction. A few more minutes passed. Finally I went up to them and asked whether it was their intention to let me in at all. I injected as much sarcasm as I could into my voice. It was my only weapon but it didn't do me any good. The man who had banished me to the corner simply looked at me from head to foot, scowled, and generally did his best to make me feel like the agent of some malignant force sent for the sole purpose of upsetting the smooth course of his day. Then he wearily pointed in the direction the other man had gone and immediately dismissed me from his consciousness. He had proved his point; there was nothing more he could do without risking the possibility of trouble.

'What do you want?' the man barked. He was sitting behind a desk and frowning at a pile of index cards. I patiently explained. I tried to impress on him that I had come all the way from London just to use his library. He listened in silence, his forehead a mass of furrows. He asked me for identification. I cursed myself for not bringing my passport along. I showed him instead my London University library ticket. He took it, scrutinized it carefully, and then said it wasn't sufficient. I was on the point of pleading with him but I knew this would be a tactical error. The exercise of power depends on reducing the intended victim to a snivelling heap. I wasn't going to give him that satisfaction.

I went to search out a member of staff, a playwright and

novelist I had met at an African literature conference in London some months before. I was working on the principle of the bigger stick, which is the only language petty officials understand. He wasn't in his office. The departmental secretary was busy sharing an elaborate joke with a friend. She kept me waiting a few minutes before she finally acknowledged my presence.

'He has travelled,' she said, before I had finished speaking, and then turned ostentatiously back to her friend.

I had had enough for one day. I went to the zoo instead. The chimpanzees were performing for the schoolchildren, who were throwing them bits of food. Their repertoire was limited. It consisted mostly of a back somersault. If that didn't produce the desired effect they would hit the bars in an amusing display of bad temper. A young couple who stood beside me were bent double with laughter.

'But God is great,' the man said, gasping for breath.

I went to Gbadebo's office. He told me I had just missed Johnny, a childhood friend of mine. Johnny was a doctor and a hopeful writer. He had come to discuss the publication of a thriller he had written. When Gbadebo told him I was in town he had invited us both to his house that evening.

Johnny, like me, is the product of what is often referred to as a 'mixed marriage', a term I detest. Our mothers had been good friends. They still are. As Englishwomen married to Nigerians in the Lagos of the 1950s they formed a highly visible and exclusive community. Very few of these marriages worked. I suspect the motives of the men. I think that many of them married Englishwomen, white women, for the status. It went along with their degrees. It was part of making it at a time when, with the country moving towards Independence, Nigerians were turning up all over the world looking for an education, a skill, a trade. When they returned home, with their English degrees and their English wives, they were allocated houses in exclusive residential districts which had formerly been the preserve of the ruling expatriate community. But what they returned to wasn't quite what they had imagined during those interminable English winters in depressing bedsits and shabby hostels. They couldn't have bargained on the isolation. Their white neighbours refused to have anything to do with them. As a child – I must have been seven or eight because my parents were still together – I remember standing at my bedroom window and looking into our neighbour's front garden. It was the middle of the afternoon. They were having a party, or so they called it. It involved people standing around in small groups and sipping delicately from tall-stemmed glasses. My parents weren't invited. They would have lowered the tone. I don't imagine that they would have wanted to attend: one simply wants to be invited. My father invited them to his parties. They were neighbours, after all. They never came. The parties my father threw were loud. He would hire a band, put up coloured lights in the garden and engage a hotel to do the catering. Men and women, dressed to kill, drank, shouted and danced all night.

It must be said that the attitudes of Nigerians toward such marriages were complex. On the one hand, there was undoubtedly much kudos to be derived from having a white wife, which meant that you were just as good as white men; on the other hand Nigerians didn't like these marriages any more than did the English. This is not racism but cultural chauvinism: it is the impulse which, combined with the necessary energy at the right historical moment, creates empires. My father was wasted on a foreigner. He had, therefore, been seeing a Nigerian woman, with everybody's approval. He even had a child by her. Well, this was Nigeria. It was the kind of thing Nigerian men did, as Nigerian women knew, and one can only guess at the kinds of pressures that were on my father to conform to the image of the successful Nigerian male, an image already compromised by his English wife, his English profession and his English neighbours. I remember him saying, countless times, 'I'm a big man, I can do what I like,' before storming off to visit his girlfriend. This was around the time of Independence, a fact which seems to me of enormous significance.

The break-up took three years. Every time they had a fight my father went and called his relations. And they came running. My father, after all, *was* a big man. To be a big man in Nigeria is not a joke. You can do many things, including intimidate policemen. One day, after a particularly vicious fight, my mother filed a complaint at the police station. As soon as the sergeant on duty heard the surname he broke into a sweat. He begged my mother to reconsider. When she refused, he apologized profusely but said he could do nothing. One needn't be harsh with this man. He only wanted to feed his family. My mother, on the other hand, didn't have her people. They lived elsewhere. She didn't even speak the language. She was a nobody.

But I have a lot of respect for the Englishwomen who gave up everything for these men. Their independence of spirit and moral courage had enabled them to take the men as they found them, to ignore the racism and the colonial rhetoric at home and to be faithful to something infinitely purer. It is they who have ended up paying the highest price of all for the colonial encounter. The world has its own logic.

Johnny, a tall, thin man with a prominent Adam's apple – one of those curious features that have a way of staying with you years after you have forgotten what the person even looked like – had also attended St Gregory's College. He had been senior perfect when I was in the third form, which made him about five years older than me. Unlike me he had remained in Nigeria. He was married to a Nigerian. His wife, Bolanle, had spent many years in England at a well-known public school. They had three children. To look at the children you would never guess that they had a white grandmother. In another generation or two she will be recalled as an exotic curiosity, if she is remembered at all.

I had been following Johnny's literary career from England. His mother had given me a copy of his novel. It was about corruption, a favourite theme of Nigerian writers. Driving home from work one night a man comes across a corpse in the middle of the road. He takes it to the mortuary, finds himself accused of murder and is eventually tried and executed. In many ways the book exemplifies the problem of modern Nigerian writing in English. The problem at the heart of this literature is one of language. Consider the following passage, taken at random, from Johnny's novel:

As he continued to look at her, she suddenly became aware of his eyes on her and looking down she realized that she was still in her towel and, the towel had slipped to reveal slightly more than she was used to letting men see even when she was in her bikini at the pool. She covered herself and looked embarrassingly at him, but Dayo had already turned away to admire the paintings on the wall which he did not really see.

Now Naimo was embarrassed at suspecting that Dayo would take advantage of her, she was also rather disappointed by the realisation that her exposed breasts had excited no more than a long stare from Dayo, who was still looking around the room. These conflicting emotions only served to confuse her the more. She made her excuses and went to put the food on the table.

The proliferation of breasts in Nigerian novels indicates what must amount to a national obession; and, yes, Dayo does get his wicked way. But it is the language that betrays the writer: he simply doesn't handle it with the ease and familiarity of the native English speaker. This is because it isn't native to the country. English, in Nigeria, is only a language of convenience: it is not a language of real communication. Take Akin, who grew up in a village in Hampshire until he was ten years old and whose profession demands a high level of competence in English. But English is not the language he uses with his family and friends. So it is with all but a tiny minority of Nigerians. So it is with Johnny. And yet he continues to write in what is essentially a foreign language. Why? Because he lacks confidence; because he has been taught to revere the achievements of a foreign tradition and to despise his own; because he prefers a bad review in the *Times Literary Supplement* to a good review in the (Lagos) *Daily Times*. For him the centre of the real literary world is London, not Lagos; the real audience is British, not Nigerian. And yet, while secretly revering the traditions of Europe, it is also incumbent on any self-respecting Nigerian to convince himself otherwise. Johnny, then, knew little or nothing of the tradition of English literature: he had heard about Shakespeare but not Marlowe; he had heard about Wordsworth but not Shelley; he had heard about Dickens but not George Eliot. He had heard about them, but he hadn't read them. They couldn't give him anything. England itself couldn't give him anything. He had spent a year in London doing some postgraduate work.

'I hated it. I never knew what people were thinking. I was always waiting for someone to make a racial comment, whether I was on the bus or in the tube or just walking along the street. Nigeria is my home. At least here nobody can tell me what's what. Sometimes a child will call me *oyinbo*, but I tell him off and his mother comes and begs me.'

I knew what he meant of course. I had been through something similar during my first years in England. His aggressive 'Africanness' was made all the more necessary by the fact of his white mother. In effect his desire to belong meant that he felt he had to disown her. When I saw his mother again, shortly after I had returned, she told me what a nightmare it had been when he was over. She said: 'He used to walk around trying to bump into people. He wanted them to give way. Can you believe that a grown man should behave like that? *He* wouldn't give way because he had to prove a point.'

Ironically, Bolanle was far more tolerant, though she didn't say much. She contented herself with providing food; and it wasn't until she wheeled in the main course – rice and chicken with fried plantain – that I realized how much trouble she had gone to for her husband's friends. It wasn't for our sake but for his: the look that came over her delicate features – she was as tall and as thin as he – was one of concern rather than impatience. God knows she must have heard it all before, but if Johnny had a problem with his identity he was fortunate in his wife.

I was back in the library early in the morning. I had my passport with me this time. The librarian at the check-in counter was surprised to see me. He grinned at me and let me pass. I was issued with a one-day ticket. That was all I needed. I was directed to yet another counter, where I was given a slip to fill in. A minion was summoned: it appeared that only library staff were permitted to enter the stacks. I was told to take a seat where I was kept waiting two hours. The man finally returned empty-handed. They didn't have any copies of the magazine. Perhaps I could check with the

National Archives in Lagos. They were bound to have them. I toyed with the idea of complaining to the head librarian, but I didn't have the energy and I didn't much care. I hadn't even wanted the assignment. I had only taken it on for the money.

3

BEN, A BLIND Nigerian friend of mine in London, had asked me to take some presents to his family in Ogbomosho, a large town not far from Ibadan on the way north. Ogbomosho was one of the important centres of missionary activity in mid-nineteenth-century Yorubaland and therefore possesses a relatively high proportion of Christians. Ben, himself a Christian, had grown up in the town until, at the age of nine, he had suddenly gone blind. As he told it he had been playing with some friends in the front yard, his mother had called him in for his lunch, and while he sat at the table waiting for his meal it was as if, he said, 'someone had drawn a curtain'.

Doctors who were consulted were baffled. There was nothing physically wrong with his eyes; there was no reason why he shouldn't be able to see. His parents, subsistence farmers, put it down to the work of an enemy. They dragged him from one native doctor to another, spent everything they had, but failed to find one with sufficient powers. In the end he was sent by the government to a special school in Lagos where he was taught, among other things, how to touch-type. When he was fourteen he won a scholarship to a boarding school in England. Now he is twenty-eight. He hasn't been back to Nigeria since. When I met him he was studying for a Master's degree at London

University. He was the only student on the course to pass with distinction.

The journey to Ogbomosho, by ordinary taxi, took two hours and cost N4. We had difficulty finding the part of town I was looking for. The driver, who was illiterate and therefore couldn't read the address, didn't understand my pronunciation. Yoruba is a tonal language in which the same word can mean half-a-dozen different things. He was also anxious to start on the return journey. We went right through the town to the other side. He finally delivered me into the hands of a group of women hawkers outside the gates of the main hospital, one of the landmarks of the town.

None of the women, who were selling food and soft drinks, spoke a word of English. But they wanted to help. One of them produced a three-legged stool and ordered me to sit down. As they conversed amongst themselves, I watched a completely naked woman wander about in a small circle grubbing in the dirt for scraps. Nobody paid her any attention.

By consulting passers-by the women finally figured out where it was I wanted to go. The youngest was delegated to escort me. She tied her baby on her back, relieved me of my bag, and hailed a taxi. We went deeper and deeper into the centre of the town, raising an immense amount of dust as we swerved this way and that to avoid potholes and pedestrians and the open gutters that ran either side of the laterite road. Many of the houses were simple one-storey buildings of mud and corrugated tin. They were packed close together with only a bare patch of red earth between them. There was very little vegetation anywhere: the predominant colour was a dull red.

By the time we came to a stop we had taken so many turns that I was thoroughly lost. We made for one of the few concrete buildings, parted the curtain over the entrance and entered. It was dark and bare inside and I could see straight through to the open kitchen at the back. We were directed by a group of children to a nearby room. An old man with white hair and a simple cloth tied round his waist lay on a mat on the concrete floor. He sat up slowly and with great difficulty. I shook his hand. He pointed to a wooden chair, the only piece of furniture in the room. The children clustered about the doorway and simply stared at me: this was undoubtedly an adventure and they weren't about to miss out on it. I started talking, explaining who I was and why I had come. He raised his hand and said something to one of the children. The child took off and presently returned with a young woman. Although she wasn't related to the family she was the only person in the vicinity who understood English. I began all over again, pausing now and then for her to translate. I'm not quite sure what I had expected at the end of my recital but it certainly wasn't the silence which followed. Was this man the father or not? Was this in fact the right house? Then the girl told me to bring out the presents. I placed them on the floor: two plastic handbags, two dressing table mirrors, a viewfinder with slides of London. Finally the letter. All the while there was complete silence. Were they disappointed? Had they anticipated more from a man who had come such a long way? I looked at the young woman. She seemed amused. Then she explained that the parents were away on the farm and wouldn't be back for a few days. I asked if it was possible to go and see them, or for somebody to be sent to get them. It seemed to me that, more than the token gifts, they would want to have a look at the person who had last seen their son. She shook her head. The farm was some distance away, about sixty kilometres.

I was still reluctant to go. I continued to sit where I was; the spectators remained where they were; the presents were left untouched at my feet. Only then did it occur to me that they might be embarrassed by the poverty of their surroundings. From their point of view London must have seemed an impossibly fabulous place. What could they offer me? But I wanted to give them a chance to question me. After a few more minutes of the same I stood up to leave. They, too, stirred. I offered my hand to the old man. Before I was through the doorway he had lain down to sleep.

There is a rider to this story. Six months later, in London, another Nigerian friend of mine, also from Ogbomosho, told me he had just been back for a short visit. He had called in at Ben's house. He had met the father. The father had told him that some time ago a visitor from England had come with a few presents and a letter but had left in a hurry. The visitor, he said, kept looking at his watch and had refused even to eat. He himself had returned from the farm shortly after the visitor had gone. He had sent people to Ilorin – the next town north and where I was headed – to try and catch him but without success. My friend said: 'He's an old, old man. He wants to see his son again before he dies. I gave them some money. It wasn't much; it was all I could afford. But it isn't money that they want. They want to see their son again. They want him to get married and produce grandchildren for them.'

On the way back to the hospital a motorcycle pulled level with the taxi. My companion leaned out of the window and shouted something to the man riding pillion. The motorcycle followed the taxi to the hospital. The pillion rider hurried over to me.

'So you know Ben?' he asked, grabbing my hand firmly. 'Where is he?'

'He's in London.'

'When is he coming back?'

'I don't know.'

'How is he?'

'He's fine. He asked me to deliver some things to his parents.'

The man turned to the woman and said something. Then, to me:

'Thank you, thank you, we are grateful. You have done well. Please greet him for us when you return. Tell him we are waiting for him. You have made us very happy. We are grateful.'

He climbed on the motorbike, waved, and they sped off in a cloud of dust.

I was given back my stool. A soft drink was pushed into my hand. The women gathered around my escort as she relayed the details of the day's adventure. From time to time one of the traders glanced at me and smiled in approval. When I finished my drink I indicated that I wanted to continue on my way.

'Ilorin,' I said. They nodded. I was about to get up when one of them pushed me down again. Presently an ancient mini-bus, jammed to capacity and with its undercarriage all but scraping the ground, turned the corner. They hailed it. I was given the conductor's seat; the conductor, a young man in filthy shorts, hung precariously out of the door for the remainder of the journey. It took us less than an hour. At Ilorin motor-park I booked a seat in a long-distance taxi to Kaduna.

Although technically still in the south one could already see the Muslim influence of the north. At the turn of the nineteenth century Ilorin was still part of the great Oyo Empire. It was one of the first states to agitate for greater autonomy by enlisting the aid of the Fulani in the north. Ilorin was successful, but the governor at the time hadn't counted on the expansionist drive of the Fulani whose avowed purpose, under their great leader Usumanu dan Fodio, was to 'dip the Holy Book in the Sea'. By 1830 Ilorin was under Fulani control and it was from here that the conquest of Yorubaland was launched. They got as far as the town of Oshogbo before they were finally halted. The most distinctive feature of the city was the huge mosque. It is one of the fears of the southerners that the north still has imperial ambitions; and as dusk fell, and we waited for the taxi to fill up, the wails of the believers could be heard from all directions.

This was to be the first of many journeys by the famous, or infamous, Peugeot 504 Estates, known either as station wagons or flying coffins depending on your sense of humour. For sheer efficiency there is no better way to travel if you propose to cover as much of the country as possible in a short period of time. One can fly, of course, and there are regular internal flights by Nigeria Airways to all corners, but I wanted to be on the ground throughout. The mini-buses and lorries are slow and uncomfortable; and one might as well forget about the trains, which are patronized only by the very poorest: I was to meet someone who had travelled by train from Maiduguri, in the far north-east, to Lagos, in the south-west – the distance between London and Warsaw – and he said it took three days. The only way the passengers could get any food during the endless delays was to raid the local farms. All in all he made it sound as close to purgatory as one is liable to experience in this lifetime. Besides, there are many places the train doesn't reach; or, where it does, it is invariably by the most circuitous route: to go from Lagos to Port Harcourt, in the east, one has to first go north to Kaduna.

It took an hour for the taxi to fill up, six passengers in all: one in front; three immediately behind; two at the back. The choice seat, and the most dangerous, is the one in front. Before we pulled out, the driver ran his fingers over the beads that hung from the rear-view mirror. I did the same with the St Christopher my wife had had blessed by a priest before I had left England. We were going to need all the help we could muster.

As soon as we were outside the city limits the driver slammed his foot on the accelerator and the speedometer did a complete circle. The wind rushed in through the open window and took my breath away. I was terrified. If we had a blow-out at this speed we were dead for sure. But I soon forgot about that when I saw what was to follow. Sitting bolt upright, chewing kola-nut to keep him awake, with one arm resting on the door and a cloth cap perched at an angle on his head, he thought nothing of overtaking articulated lorries uphill on a bend. His calculations were so fine that he allowed millimetres between the front of the lorry and the oncoming vehicle. The road itself wasn't too bad, at least on the first leg, but it was single lane either side.

The journey took seven hours, most of it in the dark, but the driver's judgment never faltered. We made only one stop, at a petrol station in a place called Kontagora, which was the half-way mark and a major junction. We grabbed something to eat, the windscreen was washed by one of the many boys wandering about with buckets of water for that purpose, the tank was re-filled and we were on the road again.

By now my terror had given way to a sense of fatalism: if I was destined to die then so be it. Short of stopping the taxi and getting out, which one passenger eventually did when his nerve finally snapped, I could only hope for the best. From time to time we passed the wreckage of recent collisions, heaps of twisted metal pushed to the side of the road, but these horrific sights didn't appear to have any effect on the driver. Speed was his livelihood. Behind the wheel of his car he was transported into another universe. I doubt he spoke more than half-a-dozen times in the seven hours it took us to reach Kaduna, and only then when it was absolutely necessary. In many ways he was a romantic figure and I couldn't help thinking there was something altogether majestic about him.

On the outskirts of Kaduna we ran into a tropical rainstorm. We had seen it from a distance in the intermittent flashes of lightning that lit up the sky for miles around. Visibility was reduced to zero. The windscreen wipers were rendered useless and we crawled along at walking pace. My relief at the end of the ordeal gave way to anxiety about where I would spend the night. I was rescued by the kind offer of the couple at the back who suggested that the remaining two passengers and I spend the night in their guest quarters. It was a three-bedroom, self-contained bungalow at the rear of the main house. As the electricity had been cut off, we were led to it through the tall green corn by a servant with a hurricane lamp.

I was woken by one of my companions before six. They were both young men about to embark on their one-year National Youth Service Corps. The NYSC, which was set up in the early 1970s, was restricted to university graduates below the age of thirty. The aim was to get skilled people to the rural areas where they were needed, and to foster understanding between members of different tribes. My companions seemed less than enthusiastic about the prospect, but without the certificate to show they had done it, they wouldn't be able to get a proper job.

I had already decided to press on to Kano, where I had the address of a publisher I had met at a book fair in London some months before. At the entrance to the motor-park I was overtaken by the taxi driver, who was on his way back to Ilorin.

The journey to Kano took two hours. I was now in the north proper. Compared to the south it seemed heavily under-populated, but this is a contentious point. No one knows the exact population of Nigeria. On the basis of the pre-Independence 1960 census it is reckoned to be anywhere between 80 and 120 million people. There used to be a fiction, which still survives in certain European quarters, that the inability of a country like Nigeria to carry out a more up-to-date census has something to do with 'traditional' African beliefs: that for the African to count his children is to place them on the same level as domestic animals and thereby invite the wrath of God. I shall have more to say about this notion of 'traditional' African beliefs later, the word 'traditional' being used loosely by European liberal observers to excuse patterns of behaviour which would otherwise be deemed as 'typical' African incompetence. But the real reason for the absence of a reliable census is political, as is so much else in modern Nigeria, fanciful theories notwithstanding: the 1963 census was rejected when it was discovered that the political dominance of the north rested on a slim majority; the 1973 census was rejected because it claimed that there were twice as many people in the north as there were in the south. In so far as the north continues to dominate the country politically there will never be a reliable census.

The impression of under-population was heightened by the facts of geography. Tropical rainforest had given way to open savannah. Compared with the south, where one roadside village ran into the next with hardly a break between them, villages in the north – round mud huts with conical straw roofs built in a semi-circle and enclosed by a high wattle fence – were separated by great empty spaces. There was little sign of life. Occasionally we would pass a solitary man driving his long-horned cattle, or an isolated group of women digging the soil, or – women again – walking barefoot along the side of the road under huge bundles of firewood. Many of these women must have been in their twenties or thirties, but they looked a good deal older: wrinkled faces, dried-up breasts, vacant stares. They were the true peasants. When they weren't working, which wasn't often, they were to be seen sitting idly outside their huts gazing into space. Their lives, to me, seemed horrendous.

As soon as I got out of the taxi at Kano motor-park, my arm was immediately seized by a young man in a torn shirt and torn trousers. He demanded to know where I was going. I made a move to pull away from him and he tried to reassure me by displaying his rotten teeth. In halting English he repeated his question. I gave him the address. He told me to follow him. It turned out he was a tout for one of the city taxi drivers who had to wait beyond the gates. I was directed to sit inside. The tout hung around, grinning inanely and probably hoping for some money. I gave him a cigarette instead. Then he pulled out a pools coupon and handed it to me.

'Mark it,' he said.

'But I don't know anything about the pools,' I said.

'Mark it, mark it,' he repeated, holding out a biro. I put down some crosses at random. As I was handing it back to him a friend of his hurried over and seized the completed coupon. He produced one of his own and copied the numbers I had marked. The tout tapped the side of his head and nodded. It was only later that I understood why.

Meanwhile a young, delicate-looking woman climbed in the back seat and lit a cigarette. She had straight black hair and fair skin. She reminded me of one of those frail Asian women who look as if they would snap as easily as a dry twig. Then the driver got in and we set off for the city centre.

It was still early in the day, which was just as well. To be in possession of an address is no guarantee that you will ever find it. The address I had been given seemed rather vague: 'Plot 876 Gyedi Gyedi, off Press Road, Kano.' I showed the driver the card. He stared at it uncomprehendingly until I realized that he couldn't read. So I said, 'Press Road', and he nodded. Eventually we arrived at France Road. He asked me

44

for the number. I shook my head and said, 'Press Road, Press Road.' He frowned. 'France Road,' he said, pointing to the sign. 'No, Press Road,' I said. He turned to the woman. She shook her head. He beckoned a passer-by and indicated for me to repeat the name. I did so. The man shook his head and continued on his way. 'France Road,' the driver said, letting out the clutch. 'What number?' he asked. 'No, not France Road, Press Road,' I shouted. 'France Road?' he said, and started searching for another street sign as if hoping that by some miracle I would discover that it was the right place after all. After we had been up and down twice I told him to let me down.

I walked for about ten minutes. I didn't have a clue where I was going. My shirt was soon soaked. I flagged down another taxi. 'Press Road,' I said, as casually as I could. 'France Road?' he queried. 'No, Press Road, Press Road,' I said. He shook his head and drove off. He had better things to do than argue with a stupid foreigner who didn't even know where he was going. I was beginning to wonder whether the road existed. If a taxi driver didn't know then who would? But this was ridiculous. Why should a man have a card printed with a non-existent address? He had seemed sane enough when he had invited me to stay with him.

I hailed another taxi. I decided on a different approach. Although it was Sunday I gave him the office address. I knew that State Road existed; I had passed it in the first taxi and it was a main road. Within minutes we were driving along it, but we couldn't find the right number. We couldn't even work out which side of the road it was supposed to be on. We went up, down, then up again. I was growing more and more despondent as the driver grew more and more impatient. By this time he had taken possession of the card. He kept scrutinizing it as though he were trying to crack a code. In the end he gave up and handed it back to me. I took a deep breath and said: 'Okay, take me to Press Road.'

'Press Road?'

'Yes.'

'Press Road,' he muttered; then, with sudden understanding, 'Ah, France Road!'

My heart sank. In desperation I called a passer-by.

'Could you please tell me where I can find Press Road?' I asked without much conviction.

'Press Road?' he repeated.

'Yes, Press Road, Press Road,' I said. He nodded, turned to the driver, and gave a few simple instructions.

'Ah, Press Road,' the driver said, nodding vigorously. I thanked the man. Press Road was just around the corner.

If I had imagined that my troubles were over I was mistaken. The address, after all, was 'off Press Road'. Gyedi-Gyedi was the name of a residential area, and it was huge. Now I had to find the house, but it was impossible to make out any sequence to the numbers. It was a new layout and many of the houses were only half-built. I paid off the driver, to his great relief, and at once delivered myself into the hands of an old man sitting on a stool outside one of the houses. He looked eager for any diversion that would relieve him of his boredom. He took the card, by now thoroughly grubby, and examined it. Then he ordered me to follow him. I congratulated myself on my stroke of luck.

His energy belied his age. He held himself erect and walked quickly and with great purpose, like a man who knew where he was going. We did a complete circle and arrived back at our starting-point. He shook his head, re-examined the card, and set off in a different direction. At one stage we came across a rather attractive woman putting rubbish into a dustbin. We showed her the card but she shook her head. She was on the point of saying something when the old man seized my arm and started dragging me

46

away. When we were out of earshot I demanded to know what he thought he was doing. I pointed out that she might have been able to make a useful suggestion, which was more than he could do. He smiled indulgently.

'You must be careful,' he said.

'What do you mean?'

'They can cheat you.'

'Who?'

'Those kind of women.'

'I don't understand . . .'

'Those women. They will cheat you. They will invite you into their house and give you food. Then they will charge you. You must be careful.'

It all sounded highly unlikely, but if it was true I couldn't see the objection. At that moment I wanted nothing more than to put up my feet. I would have gladly paid for the privilege.

I had had enough. If he didn't know the place why didn't he just say so and let me find someone who did?

'I thought you knew where we were going,' I said.

'Yes.'

'Then where is it?'

'I told you, I will take you there. Don't worry.'

By now we were back where we had started. The heat was almost unbearable. I was used to the humidity of the south; this fierce, dry heat was different.

'I'm not going any further,' I said, preparing to sulk. This only amused him.

'You think I don't know?' he said.

'That's right. All we've done so far is go for a long walk.' He laughed. I said:

'Then if you do know why haven't you taken me there?'

'Let us go and see somebody.'

'Who?'

'His uncle.'

'You mean you know the uncle of the man I'm looking for?'

'Yes.'

'Are you sure?'

'Yes.'

Of course I didn't believe him but I didn't have much choice. I prepared for another hike, but we simply crossed the road and entered a courtyard. A middle-aged man in expensive traditional dress – white cotton trousers beneath an expansive white top, delicately embroidered around the neck and the sleeves – was seeing off a visitor. I greeted him and gave him the card.

'You've come to visit him? From America?'

'No, England.'

'It's lucky you found me. He no longer lives at this address. Don't worry, my son will drive you there.'

4

BATURE HAD BEEN expecting me. He introduced me to his wife, a large, very black and very beautiful woman with sleepy eyes and a lazy manner. Beside her he appeared small and wiry and hyperactive: it was easy to imagine him sinking into her soft, ample flesh. They had two children, a boy and a girl. The girl, who was four years old, had her mother's colouring and her father's build. In common with all the girls, even at such a young age, a thin line of kohl had been applied around her eyes so that her eyes, white against her dark skin, stood out in greater relief.

In the living room of their bungalow, sparsely furnished with an assortment of easy chairs and dominated by a colour television set and video unit, were posters of Malcolm X and Franz Fanon. The bookshelf was filled with volumes with such titles as: *Towards a Progressive Nigeria*, *A Dying Colonialism* and *Political Repression in Nigeria*. I was shown into his wife's bedroom, where I was to sleep. It was a common arrangement in many Nigerian households for the husband and wife to have separate rooms.

After he had eaten Bature took me for a drive. Knowing the purpose of my journey, he was determined to give me all the help he could. The first stage was a complete tour of the city.

Kano is an ancient city, one of a small group of related

cities known as the Hausa Bakwai, or seven Hausa states. Their origin is obscured by legend: according to the chronicles, of which the most famous is *The Kano Chronicle*, they were founded some time before 1100. Kano, together with Katsina, was pre-eminent in trade; its market, constructed during the reign of its greatest King, Muhammad Rimfa (?1436–99), was the ultimate destination of the Arab caravans that travelled across the Sahara desert from Tripoli. It was still thriving four centuries later as the British explorer Hugh Clapperton, the first European to visit the city, records in his journal:

> The interior of the market is filled with stalls of bamboo, laid out in regular streets; where the most costly wares are sold, and articles of dress, and other little matters of use or ornament made and repaired. Bands of musicians parade up and down to attract purchasers to particular booths. Here are displayed coarse writing paper, of French manufacture, brought from Barbary; scissors and knives, of native workmanship; crude antimony and tin, both the produce of the country; unwrought silk of a red colour, which they make into belts and slings, or weave in stripes into the finest cotton tobes; armlets and bracelets of brass; beads of glass, coral, and amber; finger rings of pewter, and a few silver trinkets, but none of gold; tobes, turkadees, and turban shawls; coarse woollen cloths of all colours; coarse calico; Moorish dresses; the cast off gaudy garbs of the Mamelukes of Barbary; pieces of Egyptian linen, checked or striped with gold; sword blades from Malta, &c. &c.

Under Muhammad Rimfa Kano also became famous as one of the great centres of Islamic scholarship, Islam having been introduced a century earlier under the influence of the neighbouring Mali Empire, then at its height. Travelling scholars from the University of Timbuktu regularly visited the court. The best-known of these scholars was one Sheikh Muhammad al-Maghili of Tlemcen who functioned for a time in Kano as a special adviser to the king; his treatise, *The Obligations of Princes* – which insisted on the strict application of the *Shari'a* and a discussion of the problems facing a centralizing and reforming Muslim ruler – was to exert a powerful influence on the thinking of the great Fulani reformer and scholar, Usumanu dan Fodio, at the end of the eighteenth century.

'Abu Muhammad Sheikh Othman, son of Muhammad, son of Othman, surnamed Ibn Fodi, or, as he is called in Hausa, the Shehu Usumanu dan Fodio' was born in the Hausa state of Gobir, one of the original Hausa Bakwai in present-day Sokoto in the extreme north-west of the country. The Fulani, a light-skinned race of cattle nomads whose origin is still in dispute, had been settling peacefully in Hausaland since the fifteenth century. Many of them remained nomadic cattlemen and practised their own animistic religion, but a few settled in the towns where they inter-married with the local population and preached the virtues of Islam. This urban class gradually established itself as a powerful intellectual force increasingly critical of the Hausa kings who tolerated the practice of traditional Hausa religion alongside the Islamic faith. A following built up around the figure of Usumanu dan Fodio whose own treatise, *Wathiqat ahl al-Sudan*, called for a Holy War:

And that to make war against the king who is an apostate – who has not abandoned the religion of Islam so far as the professing of it is concerned, and who mingles the observances of Islam with the observances of heathendom, like the kings of Hausaland for the most part – is obligatory by assent, and that to take the government from him is obligatory by assent.

The call for the purification of Islam against the corrupt and decadent tendencies of the established dynasties was part of a widespread reformist movement affecting the entire Muslim word in this period. Such a movement has parallels in our own day. To get a glimpse of the social upheaval this kind of religious fervour entails one has only to look at the modern Maitatsine movement.

In December 1980 a group of religious fanatics, under their leader Maitatsine, went on the rampage. The 'disturbances', which resulted in over 4,000 deaths, lasted three weeks and brought the entire city to a standstill.

The Federal Government's *Report of Tribunal of Inquiry on Kano Disturbances*, published the following year, gives a good idea of the scale of the "disturbances":

Some units of the Nigeria Police were on the 8th December, 1980, reported to have been despatched to Shahuci Playing Ground in Kano City for the purpose of maintaining law and order while a so-called religious leader, known and referred to as Mallam Muhammadu Marwa, alias Maitatsine, and his band of militant followers were there preaching. As the Policemen were taking their position, they were attacked by armed followers of Maitatsine who emerged from their hiding among the crowd of onlookers and from behind kiosks and stalls situated in the vicinity. The Police lost some of their men, several of their vehicles were destroyed and some of their guns were captured by the fanatics. What initially looked like a minor civil commotion quickly escalated into full-scale rampage resulting in inestimable loss of life and limb and severe damage to property. Kano Municipality was engulfed in a bloody civil disorder and virtually brought to a standstill the economic life of the city.

The following day, and for eight days thereafter, Kano Mobile Force supported by reinforcements from some other State Commands maintained a siege of the area occupied by the fanatics.

When by 27th December, 1980, it was realised that the disturbance had assumed a degree of magnitude both in gravity and extremity and it was evident that the Police were unable to speedily and effectively contain the deteriorating situation, the President of the Federal Republic of Nigeria and Commander-in-Chief of the Armed Forces, Alhaji Shehu Shagari, ordered the use of the military. A military operation succeeded within 48 hours thereafter in arresting the situation and restoring peace and normalcy to the affected areas of Kano City.

This sounds more like an incipient civil war than a mere 'disturbance'. People remained indoors as much as possible; if you had to go out you made sure nobody could sneak up behind you: members of the sect, indistinguishable from ordinary citizens, butchered people in broad daylight without regard for the consequences. It was one of their beliefs that to die in the cause of Islam ensured the pleasure of Allah. Bature said:

'I didn't know that life could be so cheap. People were killing each other left and right. There were bodies everywhere. I'll never forget the sight of a hawker peeling an orange next to a corpse. Just peeling an orange and hoping to sell it to someone and there was a corpse no more than ten feet from where he was standing. That single image has never left my mind. It will remain with me till the day I die. It was terrible.'

We stopped outside the deserted compound where Maitatsine himself – described in the Report as '1.7 metres tall, slender, dark-complexioned, wore a goatee beard and 2 gold-plated incisor teeth in his upper jaw and also had a squint right eye' – had his headquarters and where 2,000 of his followers protected him:

53

In fact as early as the 10th April, 1980, Mr Sirajo Wudil, former Secretary to the Kano Municipal Local Government Council, had written to the Secretary, Kano State Government . . . complaining about the menace of Maitatsine's followers and the fact that he had built for himself an 'Empire' in Yan Awaki Quarters – where no doubt only his word was law. Mr Adewusi, Assistant Inspector-General [of Police] in his testimony stated also *inter-alia*: "One could safely say that they had declared their own *independent country within the enclave*". It is necessary to state that both in view of the fanatics and indeed in reality, the enclave was beyond the *de facto* jurisdiction of the authority of all arms of Government – State, Municipal and Traditional.

The extent to which it had become a law unto itself is shown by the fact that within the enclave there was an "open exhibition and display of captured rifles and the uniforms of slaughtered policemen". When the compound was finally stormed the list of weapons captured included: swords, cutlasses, spears, hooks, arrow heads, wire traps, knives, iron rods, dane guns, double barrel guns, Berretta pistols, tear smoke guns, clubs with weighted heads, axes, choppers, metal hooks, matchets.

From this enclave Maitatsine's followers terrorized the local population. Women, for instance, were abducted from the streets 'and forced to cook for them. Some of these women, especially the married ones, were subjected to untold humiliation and degradation . . . The stories narrated by these women clearly portrayed the obscene aspects of Maitatsine's life-style.'

Why married women 'especially' is unclear, but it is as well to point out that Usumanu dan Fodio's *jihad* was in part impelled by the appalling position of women under the Hausa rulers. He wrote, in *Nur al-Albab*:

. . . men treat these beings (women) like household implements which become broken after long use . . . this is an abominable crime. Alas – how can they thus shut up their wives, their daughters, and their captives in the darkness of ignorance while daily they impart knowledge to their students?

The Fulani revolution under Usumanu dan Fodio was essentially a revolution of radical intellectuals which brought in its wake a revival of learning that had been a feature of the reign of Muhammad Rimfa. Maitatsine can hardly be said to be of the same stature; again according to the Report:

Maitatsine was unrelenting in his bellicose and provocative preaching which generated a lot of animosity and fury against him from other religious sects. According to the evidence of witnesses . . . Maitatsine's preaching was tantamount to unbridled condemnation and ridicule of the sacrosanct principles and tenets of Islamic faith as accepted and practiced by Moslems. He outrageously condemned the Holy Quran and some of the teaching of Prophet Mohammed and in fact replaced Prophet Mohammed's name with his in the Holy Quran. He denigrated affluence and classified the elite as infidels. To him it was profane to wear a wrist watch, ride a bicycle or any mechanically propelled vehicle. Furthermore, he incited his followers to attack passersby who were not interested in his particular brand of unorthodox preaching.

Bature explained that the articles cited were symbols of 'Western decadence', a term I was to hear again and again, beginning with Bature himself.

Bature was a self-proclaimed Marxist. It hadn't taken us

long to get on to the subject of politics. In a country as politically volatile as Nigeria, it is a subject never far from the agenda. He had been quick to tell me that he had recently visited Cuba and been impressed by what he had seen; now he was making plans to visit the Soviet Union. I was surprised, but I shouldn't have been. As someone who had grown up in the south I had been encouraged to think of northerners as conservative and backward, even simple. In Lagos when I was a child the northerners, easily identified by their flowing white robes and their tall physique, were considered only good as nightwatchmen. In this they had a fearsome reputation: it was their habit to walk the streets with a dagger strapped to their upper arm. To understand the divide between north and south one must bear in mind the fact of Islam and the history of British rule.

The Holy War of Usumanu dan Fodio, beginning in 1804, was effectively over by 1830, by which time the Fulani had gained complete control not only of the Hausa states but almost all of what now comprises northern Nigeria. To this empire they brought an efficient civil service and a strict code of law. When the British took over, nearly a century later, it proved more convenient to rule through the existing structures of government, not least because of the limited resources available to the empire-builders – the men on the ground – at a time when successive British governments were dubious about colonial expansion. This became enshrined as the system of Indirect Rule.

The architect of Indirect Rule, Frederick Lugard, was a British soldier born in India in 1858 who was to become, successively, Commissioner for the Nigerian hinterland; High Commissioner of Northern Nigeria; Governor of Northern and Southern Nigeria; and, finally, in 1914, Governor-General of Nigeria. After his retirement in 1919 he wrote a book, *The Dual Mandate in British Tropical Africa*, which was published in 1922. His biographer,

Margery Perham, tells us that into this book "Lugard, quite unconsciously, put the whole man, character, experience and ideas." What is even more important is that Lugard was, profoundly, a man of his time. To read *The Dual Mandate* is to understand what the British were doing in Africa. This is contained at the end of the last chapter:

> As Roman imperialism laid the foundations of modern civilization, and led the wild barbarians of these islands along the path of progress, so in Africa to-day we are repaying the debt, and bringing to the dark places of the earth, the abode of barbarism and cruelty, the torch of culture and progress, while ministering to the material needs of our own civilization.

These are the words of a man who had studied the classics at public school, notably the Roman historians, and who belonged to a world which believed in the idea of human progress. It has been fashionable for a long time to sneer at this notion of Britain's civilizing mission in Africa and to accuse people like Lugard of bad faith. Lugard himself does not deny the material benefits to be gained from the exploitation of the colonies, and why should he? Empires are not philanthropic organizations; but to argue that his moral justification is merely a cloak for his material greed, if greed is the right word, is to be guilty of simplifying what was a complex event.

Lugard, who, we are told, 'knew Africa and Africans as did few men of his time', divided the inhabitants of the continent into two categories. The first comprised the 'Bantus' – the 'pure Negroes', in Lugard's phrase – who were further sub-divided into two groups: those with recognizable tribal institutions – 'advanced pagans' – and those without. The Yoruba, with their semi-divine Alafin (King) and various chiefs, as well as their nine-member council of government upon whom the Alafin depended, fell into the group of advanced pagans, one step up from those tribes which did not possess such institutions and who were therefore 'still in the patriarchal stage' in which 'the family is the unit, and even the village head has but little authority'. The drawback of the advanced pagans was the despotic nature of their rulers and the widespread practice of human sacrifice. This was because they lacked what the second category – the 'progressive communities' – possessed: the civilizing influence of 'an alien, monotheistic religion, which brought with it a written language and a foreign culture'.

The Hausa-Fulani of the north belonged to this second category, for which they had Islam to thank, though it is as well to point out that the Yoruba, along with most African tribes, were also monotheistic. But a religion without the weight of a literate culture behind it is at a disadvantage. Such a religion, without a central text and the commentaries that follow upon it, can only ever remain localized and marginal, the preserve of a highly specialized priestly class who must transmit it orally from one generation to the next.

It was enough, therefore, for the British to demonstrate their superiority in a series of military expeditions – notably against Sokoto and Kano in 1903 – and then simply allow the Emirs to continue as before but under the direct supervision of the British Governor.

This meant, amongst other things, the absence of missionary activity. Missionaries, who had been active in southern Nigeria for upwards of half-a-century before colonization, had been excluded from the north for obvious reasons. It was one of the conditions of subjection to British rule that this state of affairs continue. Lugard, who had no great love for the missionaries and much respect for Islam, was more than willing to go along with this. He was even contemptuous of the products of these mission schools, and it wasn't long before he turned his attention to their reform:

> Education has brought . . . only discontent, suspicion of others, and bitterness, which masquerades as racial patriotism, and the vindication of rights unjustly withheld. As citizens they are unfitted to hold posts of trust and responsibility where integrity and loyalty are essential, or to become leaders of their own community in the path of progress . . .

But it was these 'uppity' Africans who were also beginning to travel overseas to study medicine and law and engineering – my father was simply part of a long line – and generally acquire the necessary skills for the running of a modern state. This was the new source of power, and it was to have tremendous consequences for the future of the country. The north, to put it crudely, was quickly left behind, the irony being that it was precisely the absence of literacy among the tribes of the south that brought about this state of affairs. When Independence was finally achieved it was the result of southern agitation: Independence would have come sooner but for the reluctance of the nothern representatives. And it was southerners who largely took over the running of the state.

Not that I knew any of this when I was growing up in Lagos; but I was, after all, the child of a Western-educated Yoruba Christian, of whom Lugard had written:

> The Europeanized African differs not merely in mental outlook from the other groups, but also in physique. Doctors and dentists tell us that he has become less fertile, more susceptible to lung trouble and to other diseases, and to defective dentition – disabilities which have probably arisen from in-breeding among a very limited class . . .

The notion of northern backwardness was taken absolutely for granted in such households. Such prejudices, imbibed so early, are not easily discarded. Akin, who has himself travelled extensively in the north, said of his nightwatchman: 'They may be stupid but at least they're faithful.' And when I returned to Lagos he wanted to know whether I hadn't found 'them' dirty. I was astonished, but I shouldn't have been. It was what he had been taught to believe, the evidence of his own eyes notwithstanding, just as we had both been taught that the north was backward, and backwardness did not include an acquaintance with a sophisticated political philosophy.

I raised the usual objections to Marxism: that it applied to another time and another place; that it was simply the reverse side of the European political coin; that its belief in progress and science, both of which are synonymous, implied African inferiority. But all this was beside the point. Bature's political position was a consequence of his anti-Westernism. At one point, as we had been driving around, he had suddenly burst out: 'Religion provides the answer to everything. I'm glad of the world-wide resurgence of Islam and what Khomeini did to the Americans.' I could sympathize with that, just as I could sympathize with the contempt with which he regarded me as I argued against him. To him I was just another Westernized African seduced by European decadence. As Johnny knew only too well, both my accent and my colour already made me a dubious customer. But why had he been so quick to dismiss the Maitatsine movement as 'unimportant' and 'composed of riff-raff'? He wasn't going to be drawn. Instead he drove me to see a friend of his, a social science lecturer at the university.

His friend lived in a flat in a purpose-built, six-storey apartment block owned by the university. It was one of a dozen such blocks on the outskirts of the city, and in the failing light the place had a desolate air about it, partly because it had only too obviously been built on the cheap, partly because nobody had bothered to landscape the surroundings: piles of broken breeze block lay scattered in the mud, and we had to pick our way around the stagnant puddles.

The walls of his living room were adorned with posters of Walt Disney cartoon characters; his bookshelves were jammed with cheap paperbacks of the Mickey Spillane and James Hadley Chase variety; a Pink Floyd album was on the stereo.

'Do you like this music?' he asked as soon as we sat down. I shook my head. He was ironing a shirt. Naked to the waist, the sweat was pouring down his face and chest. He was a short man, rather ugly, with one of those beards that start under the chin and go half-way down the neck.

'That's the trouble. Nobody likes the music I like. Look at my record collection: only European electronic music. Have you heard the latest Pink Floyd album? I think it's fantastic. I want to get it but you can't buy it here. These people are ignorant. They only want to listen to native music. They aren't interested in what's going on elsewhere. I'm so isolated. I was born into the wrong society. I have no intellectual companionship here, not even at the university. I'm a hippie at heart, to tell the truth. I want to live in Europe or America.'

He turned off the iron and examined his shirt for creases.

'So you're a writer,' he said. Bature had announced me as such. I would have preferred it if he hadn't – I would have preferred to remain more anonymous – but his intentions were generous and I didn't have the heart to tell him.

'I suppose you've read a lot of African literature?' he said. Before I could respond he went on:

'I haven't. I don't like it. I tried an Achebe novel once because people kept pestering me but I soon got bored with it. I much prefer what you would call third-grade American sex-and-violence novels. In fact, if you really want to know, I don't believe in all this nonsense about good and bad literature. It's all the same as far as I'm concerned. I don't think you can say Tolstoy is better than Spillane.' He paused, then: 'Yes, I can see you think it's funny. Don't worry, you're not alone. Lots of other people think it's funny too. I don't care.'

He was working hard at pretending to be calm and rational but it was impossible to overlook his agitation.

'I hate this country. You know what happened once? Let me tell you how far people in this country will go for money. A woman allowed herself to be fucked by a dog in front of a crowd of people for one thousand naira. Can you believe that?'

It was impossible to verify a story like this, but in Nigeria it certainly wasn't far-fetched. One has to go to Nigeria to see the power of money. Still, it didn't strike me as sufficient reason for condemning an entire country. Nor did it explain what had gone wrong with him, why he hated his black skin and his Nigerian heritage, which is what this was all about. However much I might have disagreed with Bature, I could at least respect his position: it even occurred to me that by bringing me here Bature was trying to make me understand that any other position was untenable. This man was insane.

'What kind of music do you like?' he asked. My silence was disturbing him. Bature, who hadn't uttered a word since our arrival, had long since retreated into the newspaper.

'Jazz,' I answered.

'Then you'd like to meet my black American neighbours, colleagues of mine at the university. They're crazy about jazz.'

My curiosity was immediately aroused. It would be interesting to hear what they had to say, and I couldn't see much point talking with this man. I had taken Bature's point.

The woman wore a long skirt; her dreadlocks were covered with a scarf. The only other person I had seen with locks in the country was in Lagos, a young man in jeans and T-shirt who wouldn't have looked out of place in Brixton but who, judging by the interest he was arousing from the people nearby, was regarded as something of a curiosity.

It turned out that she was a Muslim, though I can't remember how we got on to the subject. Being in an argumentative mood, and out of genuine curiosity, I asked her whether she didn't find Islam reactionary: didn't it mean the subjugation of women? Not at all, she said; Islam merely acknowledged that men and women were different.

'It's one thing to say they're different; it's quite another to say that they're unequal,' I said. Bature was having none of it. What did I mean by saying that Islam subjugated women? Hadn't I seen his wife? She was free to do as she wanted, providing she conducted herself properly and fulfilled her obligations as a married woman.

'So she's only free within certain limitations?' I said.

'But I also have obligations. Perhaps in Europe married couples do as they like, but everybody knows Europe is decadent.' I had been hearing rather too much about European decadence, and I was to hear a lot more. I for one didn't know that Europe was decadent, but I let it pass. I recounted, instead, my own experience of Islam. It was in an inner-city Birmingham slum a few years ago. More than half the residents on our street were first-generation immigrants from Bangladesh. The women were only ever seen on the streets dressed in full purdah and then mostly at night as they scuttled across the road to visit a friend. They weren't even permitted to collect milk from the doorstep. The milkman delivered the milk inside the front door, for which purpose he had been provided with a key to each of the houses. It happened that one of my daughters was friendly with a Bengali girl her age who attended the same school.

63

On her twelfth birthday she was suddenly removed from school and forbidden to go out. One day we heard that she was engaged to be married to a man she had never met.

'That has nothing to do with the true practice of Islam. They have perverted the teachings of the prophet,' Bature said when I had finished. 'You've made the mistake of judging a religion on the basis of an extreme example. You're not the first to do so.'

I understood what he was driving at: the example *was* extreme. It is hardly surprising that such a community, finding itself washed-up in an alien culture, should attempt to compensate by going over the top. And after all there was a connection between what I was doing here and what Europeans have been doing to Africa for centuries. How often does it happen that Europeans go out of their way to unearth an isolated community deep in the bush in order to make general statements about the African way of life? It never occurs to them that they might be observing an aberration, that your average Lagosian, trying to hustle a living in the modern city, would find them just as strange, just as exotic. The truth is always more prosaic, certainly less glamorous, especially if one were to suggest that such a community, because isolated, is actually irrelevant: it has no power; it doesn't dictate the forces that matter. But then Europe has a great need for an Africa that is a mystery, an Africa which represents the unknown, the dark side of Europe itself: such an Africa is a myth in the proper sense, which is why it shouldn't be taken altogether seriously by Africans. It has little to do with the real Africa.

But I still wasn't satisfied.

'So you don't have ultimate power over your wife?' I asked.

'Not at all.'

'What if you disagree with her over something?'

'We try and reach a compromise.'

'But that isn't always possible. What if you sincerely believe she's in the wrong?'

'Then I correct her.'

'How?'

'By telling her.'

'And if she still disagrees?'

'Then I'm permitted to impose a certain amount of physical punishment.'

'By beating her?'

'Not exactly.'

'Then how?'

'I can rap her lightly on her knuckles.'

'And you see nothing strange about that? Isn't that the way one treats children who have done wrong?' I turned to the woman: 'Do you agree with that?'

'Yes, I do. Do you find that strange?'

'Frankly, yes. You're an American. Women in America have fought hard for equality.'

'And look at the state of America,' she burst out. 'I grew up in New York. It's not safe to walk the streets. Everyday women are raped in broad daylight and nobody does anything about it. People are stabbed to death on the subway and everybody pretends it's normal. America is a sick society.'

'Exactly, and you seem to be idolizing it,' Bature said.

'Equally terrible things happen here in Nigeria,' I said. 'People are murdered in their beds by armed robbers; innocent people are whipped in the street by the police. So what? To merely state the facts explains nothing.'

The husband had all the while remained silent, but I could see he was unhappy about his wife's easy complacency. While she served us beer and popcorn I turned to him:

'What disturbs me about Nigeria is this hierarchy. I don't just mean the position of women, or about the north only. It

65

exists in the south as well, though perhaps not to the same degree.' I recounted an incident during my last visit. I had stayed in my uncle's house. A wealthy businessman, he employed a sixteen-year-old houseboy to cook and clean. My uncle was away on one of his trips for the first two weeks I was there. The boy was supposed to come in every day and clean the house. After the first few days he took to sleeping in one of the bedrooms. Once I came home and found him stretched out on the sofa with the record player on full volume. He didn't even bother to move when I entered. He had taken me for a fool and in his eyes he was right. Because I didn't assert my authority, because I didn't shout at him and push him around, he couldn't function properly. He was only a servant, a nobody. When my uncle returned the house was in a mess. He called the boy and beat him up, but it was my fault and we all knew it. I spoke to the boy later, I was trying to be kind but I was wasting my time. There was nothing like resentment on his features, no consciousness that his person had been violated. His servility was complete. Since my uncle paid him he could do what he liked to him.

'My point is this,' I said, warming to my theme: 'Such a society has no room for individual initiative and ambition. These are dangerous qualities for a person to possess, but they are the very qualities which move a society. It seems to me an important feature of American society and it must account in some way for its dominant position in the world, for the fact that every time the dollar goes up or down everybody has to take notice. Without that push and drive a society stagnates. It leaves itself wide-open to conquest by a more vigorous and dynamic society.'

The John Coltrane album came to an end at the same time as I stopped talking. There was a short silence before Bature looked at his watch and suggested we leave. The couple were relieved, especially the woman. She had escaped the horrors of America for the sanctuary of Africa, and here I was trying to rock the boat.

The following morning Bature took me along with him to his office. He was anxious for me to meet some of his colleagues. Unfortunately they were all too busy. By mid-morning, thoroughly bored, I went for a walk. I had some postcards I wanted to send to England.

On my way to the post office I passed through one of the meat markets. The trade here was entirely in the hands of men, unlike in the south where it is dominated by women. If I had to live there I would become a vegetarian. The place was filthy. Great slabs of meat, exposed to the sun on dirty squares of plywood, had attracted every fly in the city. Now and then the seller would swot at them but to little effect. On either side of the road the open gutter ran with blood from the slaughter. Every time a vehicle passed clouds of fine red dust were thrown into the air.

Back in the office I was left on my own while Bature attended a meeting. I stood at the window and watched the activity outside. A young man was giving a Kung Fu demonstration to some friends; a blind old man, a stick in one hand and a begging bowl in the other, was being led by a small boy; a completely naked man with matted hair was standing on the island in the middle of the road chuckling to himself. And there were hawkers everywhere selling everything from soft drinks to cooked food to rubber slippers to complete suits. Many of them were children, some not much more than ten years old.

Bature returned. He had a letter in his hand. It was a programme for the 10th Ife Book Fair, to be held at the university on November 7-10. Also enclosed was an application form for a stall. The closing date to apply was August 5. Today was August 11. The letter had only just arrived. We went home for lunch.

I decided to leave for Zaria the following day. It was one of the advantages of travelling the way I was that I could decide to up and go at a moment's notice. I had been given the address of an Englishman who taught at the university there.

Bature was disappointed. He wanted me to stay a day or two longer, but when he saw I was determined he suddenly became very solemn and said:

'Please, write objectively about what you've seen. Bear in mind that although Nigeria has tremendous problems we Nigerians are not despairing. We are hopeful that great things will be done. I can't wait to read your book. I'm sure it will be a great success.' His wife made me promise that next time I came I would bring my wife so she could take her to see her friends. Before I left they insisted I take some pictures of them and their two children.

5

To get to Zaria meant doubling back the way I had come. I should really have stopped off there on my way to Kano but I hadn't bothered to check my map before leaving Kaduna.

I found Michael without much difficulty. Although the university was on vacation he was chairing a seminar. A tall, sallow, fair-haired man, he seemed grateful for the interruption and pleasantly surprised to see me. He knew my work from *London Magazine*. All the same I was lucky to catch him. He was off to Kano that same afternoon on university business.

He drove me to his place in his battered Volkswagen and introduced me to 'the boys'. They would look after me until he returned in a couple of days. 'The boys' were Ivan, his eighteen-year-old son by his first marriage, and Terry, Ivan's best friend.

He lived in an open-plan, colonial-style bungalow owned by the university. The porch led into a large sitting room which was separated from the dining room on the left by an arch. A door on the right led into the master bedroom, through which you had to pass to get to the bathroom and Ivan's room. The kitchen was off the dining room.

The bungalow had the feel of a bachelor's quarters: the unmade beds, the dusty books, the sock under the settee, the dirty plates in the kitchen sink. It had the transient quality of all such households, as if the occupants were daily expecting to move on. I guessed that he and his son lived alone. I was surprised. I knew, from the blurb on a collection of his poetry I had read, that he had re-married, this time to a Nigerian. I noticed a photograph of a Nigerian woman above the makeshift bed in the living room where I was to sleep. He said they had recently separated. Before he could elaborate a car pulled up outside and a young man entered. He was one of Michael's research students who was to drive him to Kano, and he was anxious to be on his way.

Ivan and Terry, who had kept out of the way until now, suggested we drive into town and pick up some food. Before he left Michael had offered me the use of his car, but when I told him that I didn't drive he had left instructions with Terry that he was only permitted to use it to take me out. Under no circumstances was he to go out in it by himself. At first I was inclined to think he was fussing unnecessarily – he gave the impression of a man who fussed – but I soon understood his fears. There was a quality of recklessness about Terry which quickly revealed itself.

We bolted along at full speed to a nearby hotel. It was early afternoon, extremely hot, and I fancied a swim. I didn't have any swimming trunks with me. Terry, who knew the manager, procured a pair for me. It was typical of Terry that he also knew the only other people there, two girls sitting on the edge of the pool. They had been watching us more-or-less openly ever since we had arrived. Terry invited them over, ordered drinks all round, made sure there was nothing else I wanted, and then announced he was off to the market and would be back soon. I wasn't fooled. I knew very well that he was being attentive in order to be able to do what he wanted, which was to exploit the freedom of Michael's absence. Life had taught him that everything has a price. He wanted me to like him. What he didn't realize, or couldn't allow himself the luxury of suspecting, was that I understood the syndrome only too well. From the few hints he had deliberately thrown out it was clear that the circumstances of his life had demanded that he take nothing for granted – least of all that he could be liked for his own sake. And what had he told me? That he was twenty-two; that he had no qualifications; that his Scottish mother had long since returned home; that he didn't get on with his father and stepmother. I could identify with him, which is why he interested me.

The contrast with Ivan was striking. Tall, thin, anaemic-looking, his face covered with adolescent spots and a few whiskers that passed for a moustache, Ivan had instinctively chosen the corner seat where he was partially hidden by the overhanging foliage. He said little and giggled often, speaking only when spoken to and covering his mouth when he did so. To say that he was shy and self-conscious would be an understatement: he was like one of those hypersensitive creatures that curl into a ball the moment you poke it. I poked him here and there and managed to elicit some information: that his mother, whom he hadn't seen in six years, lived in America; that he hated England, where he had recently spent an abortive year living with his grandparents in Tunbridge Wells; that he was now studying for his 'A' levels by correspondence. All this was teased out of him in dribs and drabs. The girls, meanwhile, were sharing an elaborate joke and kept clutching at each other. It seemed to involve an Indian film they had seen the day before. For some reason I have never been able to understand Indian films are popular in Nigeria, especially in the cheap, open-air cinemas. One of the girls was pretending to be the heroine. She was an unlikely Indian princess: she had deep tribal marks on each cheek, a sight which is still fairly common among more traditional Nigerians, particularly in the rural areas. The display was all for our benefit, but wasted. I hadn't wanted them to join us in the first place. I spent most of the time in the pool.

Terry was away a long time. He returned in the late afternoon with two friends: a young woman he introduced as his 'sweetheart', and Jimoh, a young man of about his age with handsome, if brutal, good looks. They sat at the bar, where Terry was holding court. He worked hard for his living, such as it was. I took him aside and asked him if there was a place we could buy some marijuana. If I was to be condemned to their company for the next two days I could at least get stoned.

We drove some distance out of town, five of us crammed into the small car, and then turned off the main road. We followed a narrow path between the corn until we came to a solitary figure chewing nonchalantly on a blade of grass. He could have been expecting us. Terry spoke to him, the man disappeared into the plantation, and returned a few minutes later with a fistful of small white bundles. When the transaction was completed the man said:

'Any bettah for me?'

'Tomorrow,' Terry said and started reversing. He hit a puddle at the same moment as two men pulled level with us. One of them was badly splashed, his clean, cream-coloured trousers muddied from the knees down. He let out a curse and Terry slammed on the brakes. Terry got out and hurried over to them, ignoring his girlfriend's pleas. Jimoh chuckled and shook his head: 'That boy likes trouble,' he said approvingly. There was nothing for it. I reluctantly got out but it was already clear that neither of the men wanted a fight. Words were exchanged, Terry pressed home his advantage, and returned to the car. As we drove off he said: 'I don't mind people insulting me but when they drag in my father it's another matter.'

'You should have let it drop,' I said; 'it's hardly ever worth it.'

"Why?' he exploded. 'Why should I? If they have an argument with me, fine, but why mention my family?'

Back at the bungalow Ivan made himself scarce while Terry took charge. Within an hour he emerged from the kitchen with plates of rice and chicken. He was a good cook.

Later in the evening, after Terry's girlfriend had gone home, we went to a night club. On the way we stopped to pick up Terry's older brother, Kola, and his brother's wife, Ola.

Ola was an ample woman, big-breasted, big-bottomed, not exactly attractive to look at but soft and yielding. She had a provocative way of walking, rather slow and lazy, jutting out her behind and swaying from side to side. That evening she was sulking, her mouth pursed in a pout. Kola ignored her.

Jimoh entertained us with a story. It concerned a certain wealthy Alhaji whose wife came upon him in a restaurant with his mistress. In a fit of rage she emptied his dinner over his lap, whereupon the frightened mistress prepared to leave. The Alhaji ordered her to remain where she was and called the waiter to bring the same again. He ate slowly while his wife, sitting at an adjoining table, stared at them. Afterwards he drove his mistress to her place, his wife following behind. Then he went home and turned on her. He made it clear that what he did outside his house was entirely his own affair and that he would not tolerate such 'embarrassment' again. Then he told her to pack her belongings and leave, at which point she fell on her knees and begged his forgiveness.

Kola roared with approval; Ivan covered his mouth with his hand and sniggered; Ola pursed her lips even harder.

Jimoh continued. His own father had been like that. His mother had been so scared of him that she didn't dare say anything even when her husband drove up to the house with one of his mistresses and left her in the car while he got changed. She had no right to complain as long as she was well provided for, as long as she was fed, clothed and housed and had her children for company. A man needs many women; a woman needs only one man: as long as the man doesn't actually bring one of his mistresses into the house, 'which would be to indirectly insult her', he has done nothing reprehensible. And a woman secretly respects such a man, however much she may protest. In any case, now that his father is an old man and no longer has the stamina to chase after women his wife has him all to herself. That is the reward for her patience.

Kola nodded vigorously and elbowed Ola in the ribs. 'You hear that?' he said triumphantly. She looked him up and down, a murderous glint in her eyes.

'I don't think that's good enough,' I said. 'I know for a fact that the woman suffers. My own father carried on like that and my mother suffered for it.'

Jimoh smiled indulgently and said nothing. Kola called for more drinks. Ola announced that she was going to the toilet. She headed towards the entrance.

'Where does that stupid bitch think she's going?' Kola said and hissed at her. She ignored him. He yelled at her and pointed impatiently in the opposite direction. She pretended she had made a mistake and set off in her provocative, smouldering way, swinging her hips and jutting out her breasts. She was wasting her time. Kola and Jimoh were huddled together swopping anecdotes. Terry had long since disappeared, only God knew where. Ivan was morosely staring at his intertwined fingers, a foolish grin on his face. All of a sudden the heavens opened and it began belting down, as it had been threatening to do.

Because it was midweek the club was virtually empty. When Terry finally returned we decided to leave. His idea was to pick up some beers from Kola's place and return to the bungalow for an impromptu party. I wasn't keen: I

74

knew Michael would have disapproved and in any case I was tired. I had been up since early morning and I wanted nothing more than to go to bed with a book. As I was sleeping in the sitting room I would be forced to stay up until everyone else decided to turn in. That didn't seem likely for a few hours yet.

The secondary roads, which were really just dirt lanes, had turned into swamps. It was impossible to gauge the depth of the potholes. The car finally got stuck. We piled out and started to push. Within seconds we were soaked to the skin. I had foolishly positioned myself behind one of the back tyres. When the car roared off I was spattered with mud. It was all I could do to keep my temper in check.

Kola and Ola had meanwhile gone on ahead. As soon as we entered their parlour it was clear that matters had deteriorated further. Ola was leaning against the makeshift wooden bar, her arms folded across her chest, her pout replaced by a scowl. Kola looked as if he was about to hit her.

'Let's go,' Terry said.

'This bitch says she doesn't want to come,' Kola said.

'Is that true? Why not?' Terry demanded.

She didn't answer.

'Idiot!' Kola said and pushed her aside. He opened the fridge and counted two bottles each. He distributed them amongst us and started for the door.

'For the last time I'm telling you to come,' Kola said.

'Who are you telling? Who?' she snapped.

'Leave her and let's go,' Terry said.

We got back in the car.

'Wait!' Kola screamed as Terry began reversing. He scrambled out. We waited awhile, then Terry continued reversing. We had gone some way down the road when the pair of them emerged. Terry didn't see them; it was Jimoh who told him to stop. Kola trudged towards us, Ola following reluctantly behind. They climbed in.

'Why were you going?' Kola demanded.

'Because you can't keep your woman in line,' Terry said. Ivan sniggered. We drove the rest of the way in silence.

Back at the bungalow Terry and Kola set about preparing food. Ola sulked in one corner; Ivan chewed his fingers in another. Jimoh, a bottle of beer in one hand and a joint in the other, paced restlessly up and down glancing at the titles on the bookshelves. I lay on the bed. I doubted I would be able to stay awake much longer. Jimoh came and sat beside me.

Apropos of nothing he told me a story. A certain man bought a hotel and gave it over to his brother to manage for him. With the hotel came a fleet of twenty cars. The brother sold off four of the cars and went into the hotel business himself. While he was building up his own business he let his brother's hotel go to the wall.

He told me another story. A certain man employed his brother to build a storey house. The brother built a bungalow as well as the house. When both buildings were completed he went to his brother and announced that he was keeping the house for himself and that he had tied it all up legally. Enraged, the man took the matter to the family. They begged him not to go to the authorities even though there was nothing they could do. The only course left open was for him to swallow his anger and wash his hands of the whole affair. Now the other is riding around in a brand new Mercedes. Jimoh said: 'Any relative of mine who entrusts his business to me is making a serious mistake which he will regret as long as he lives.' On that note he got up and wandered off to the kitchen. Ivan followed him. As Ivan passed Ola she said, cruelly: 'He walks as if he has an egg in his anus.' It was true. He had a peculiar, jerky way of walking: he kept his back stiff and he didn't bend his knees, like a man who was uncomfortable with his body.

They left early the next morning. Only Jimoh remained behind. He opened a bottle of beer for breakfast and we talked in a desultory sort of way as we waited for Ivan and Terry to return. That is to say Jimoh talked and I listened. He had two subjects: women and money.

He once had a girlfriend who tried to trap him into marriage by claiming she was pregnant by him. He pretended to be pleased and promised to marry her. Then he explained that since he came from a royal family they would have to travel to his hometown to consult the oracle. There was nothing to be worried about; it was merely a formality. Then they would be free to marry. But, he warned, if there was even the remotest possibility that she was lying the consequences could be serious. She might even die. He never saw her again.

He told me another story, about another girlfriend who tried to play the same trick on him. As with the first he pretended to be pleased. That same evening he took her to a party. He danced only with her and made sure she had plenty to drink. Then he drugged her. After she had fallen unconscious a doctor friend, who had already been alerted, aborted the foetus. In the morning all she saw was a trace of blood. Two weeks later she had her period.

Later in the morning a middle-aged man turned up. He was powerfully built, wore dark glasses, and introduced himself as Muhammad. He asked whether Michael was back, and then went off to change. I later saw him in an old pair of trousers cutting the grass at the back. Michael had told me about him before he had left. He had been a civil servant until he had been retrenched as part of the government's drive to reduce the size of the public sector. Michael employed him to look after the grounds, which were extensive.

Jimoh and I went for a drink at the nearby clubhouse. He told me yet another story.

There was an Alhaji who was so wealthy he didn't know what to do with his money. Every night he had a different woman. He would drive along the road, stop beside a woman he liked the look of, and tell her to name her price. Strictly no frills: subtlety didn't come into it. And it never failed. Once, when Jimoh was with him, he picked up two women and booked into a hotel. They all shared a double-bed. The Alhaji never let up all night. 'Just like a dog,' Jimoh said.

We returned in the early afternoon. The clothes I had washed before we left were bone dry. Muhammad appeared to have finished for the day. He was sitting on the porch typing a letter with two fingers. Jimoh looked at him with disgust.

Thoroughly bored by Jimoh's company, and enervated by the heat, I sat at Michael's desk in the dining room and rolled a sheet of paper into his portable typewriter, one of those big, old-fashioned office typewriters, heavy, solid and slow. I began typing Jimoh's anecdotes. It made a change from writing in longhand, which I dislike. I was on the second sheet when Jimoh came over with a bottle of beer and started reading over my shoulder. It didn't occur to him that one didn't do this; it didn't occur to me that he would have thought it quite natural: there was no getting away from him. He looked slightly baffled and a little hurt, as though he had caught me in an act of betrayal, but said nothing. He wandered off but I didn't continue. Nor did he tell me any more anecdotes.

Ivan and Terry arrived back shortly afterwards. Presently Muhammad announced that he wanted to go. When nobody responded he simply went back to his seat on the porch.

'Who does he think he is?' Terry said angrily.

'Does your father usually run him back?' I asked Ivan. Ivan, who was busy staring at the floor, nodded his head.

'Then I think you had better do so,' I said to Terry.

78

'He's only a houseboy; he works here,' Jimoh said, loudly enough for Muhammad to hear. 'Anyway, he's too proud,' he added.

'Maybe it's all he's got left,' I said. But it wasn't that Terry and Jimoh didn't understand: it was that they were too young and too Nigerian. One simply didn't allow oneself the luxury of pity. If Muhammad had fallen on hard times that was his lookout. Whatever he had been before was of no interest. He was now a gardener, 'a houseboy'. You didn't drive your gardener home unless you were an Englishman with liberal ideas. To do so would be to jeopardize your social position and blur the distinction between you and the man you employed.

Since Terry couldn't refuse to do what I told him – I was his elder – he did the next best thing, which was to keep the man waiting. And Muhammad waited, staring into the distance through his sunglasses and not saying a word. At least he could comfort himself with the knowledge that Terry was also the object of Michael's charity. When, finally, Terry obliged, he put his head round the door and politely bade me goodbye.

Terry busied himself the following morning washing the car, berating Ivan all the while for not helping. He finished just as Michael drove up with his research student. I was pleased to see him. I was in need of adult company.

As we drank beer and he unwound he told me about himself. He said he was 48 and the only child of his parents. His father had been a small businessman; his mother, an alcoholic, was once a moderately successful singer of popular songs.

He went to university late, in his mid-twenties, and then taught for two years in a college of education in the north of England. It was while teaching there that he had married his first wife. She was also a poet and an academic; she had done

79

a Ph.D on the Danish philosopher, Søren Kierkegaard. They took out a mortgage on a semi-detached.

He quickly became disillusioned with the life he was living: 'It wasn't going anywhere. Just more of the same stretching out indefinitely.' I understood what he meant. It was easy to picture the semi-detached in Leeds and the dreary bourgeois lifestyle that goes with it.

His marriage started to crumble. One day he came across an ad in the paper for teachers in Nigeria. He thought that a fresh start in a foreign country might solve his problems. He was both right and wrong. His wife hated Nigeria: 'She was heavily into the women's movement and she couldn't accept the inferior status of women here. I can't say I blamed her.' That was in 1970. His wife left after only a year but he stayed on. He liked the life – the freedom, the easy pace, the informality – which was in such contrast to the life he had known.

Left with a child to bring up he decided he needed to get married again. It was a cold-blooded decision. One day he met a prostitute in a Kano hotel. She had lost both her parents early in life, had been adopted by an older woman, and had 'fallen into the sort of life you might expect'.

He liked her immediately. Soon afterwards they got married. She had no money sense, which was a constant source of friction between them. She was also insanely jealous of intellectual women. When he had met her she was illiterate. He had taught her to read and write. I had seen the results in an exercise book I had come across. It was filled with childish scrawls. They had stayed together for thirteen years. She was now living with friends in town. He was disappointed they had broken up: 'I feel a sense of failure. It was my second attempt. I wanted it to work.'

At the moment she was trying to run some sort of business. He was sceptical. He hoped she wouldn't drift back into the life she had been living before: she would get hurt sooner or later. Prostitutes in the north, challenging as they do every concept of the 'virtuous' woman, could be beaten with impunity. Her surrogate mother, who was still in the business, had recently been stabbed through the cheek in the back seat of a taxi and had lost an eye as a result.

I wasn't surprised by the alacrity with which Michael had opened up. I have become used to it. You only have to ask and people will tell you the most incredible details of their personal life. But talking so much left him agitated. We decided to go to a bar. On the way we collected a friend of his who lived nearby, a colleague at the university.

I liked Ade at once. He was an unhappy man. He had good reason. His wife, a chemistry teacher, was expecting their fifth child in eight years, and only the other day a 'cousin' of his had turned up on his doorstep without warning. The cousin had just finished school and wanted to go to university, so the family sent him to Ade as the only one who knew about these things. He said: "That's the extended family for you. People never take things like this into account when they praise it." He could hardly explain that he was only a junior lecturer, that he wasn't responsible for admissions, and that in any case the boy wasn't sufficiently qualified. So he was unhappy, and grateful for the opportunity to escape. If we stayed in the bar longer than we had intended it was because of him.

Ade taught politics. I asked him what he thought about Maitatsine. He shrugged: 'A bunch of fanatics. They aren't important.' But he gave an interesting explanation of why Maitatsine was able to operate outside the law for so long. The northern political elite, the so-called Kaduna Mafia – defined as 'a cohesive amalgam of Northern politicians, intelligentsia, top bureaucrats, managers, investors, gentlemen farmers, military and police commanders' – believed that he possessed magical powers.

81

Ade was more concerned with the worsening political climate. It had become impossible to criticize the military government without being branded a Marxist. Now when people gathered together they talked 'nonsense and abstractions' for fear of being overheard by members of the Nigerian Security Organization (NSO). And if you were reported you could be charged under Decree 4, 'Public Officers (Protection Against False Accusation) Decree':

> Any person who publishes in any form, whether written or otherwise, any message, rumour, report or statement . . . which is false in any material particular or which brings or is calculated to bring the Federal Military Government or the Government of a State or a public officer to ridicule or disrepute, shall be guilty of an offence . . .

Trial was by military tribunal. Civilian judges were present only in an advisory capacity. The maximum sentence was two years' imprisonment.

The proliferation of decrees under the military was alarming. The notorious Decree 20: 'Special Tribunal (Miscellaneous Offences) Decree', made it a capital offence to tamper with oil pipelines, commit arson or deal in cocaine. The Decree was so miscellaneous that it even included a 21-year prison sentence for exam cheating. Public execution by firing squad had been carried out until recently. I had spoken to someone who had witnessed one of these executions. The mental picture I had was of a swift, orderly affair. It wasn't like that, he said. The soldiers were bad shots. The bullets tore into the flesh and there was blood everywhere. In the end the commanding officer had to go up to each of the three condemned men in turn and shoot at point-blank range. It was held on the beach in Lagos. Hawkers sold ice-cream and soft drinks to the thirsty onlookers. Those who couldn't attend, or preferred their domestic comforts, could watch the proceedings on television.

As he painted a gloomier and gloomier picture he became more and more despondent. The more despondent he became the more he drank. By early evening he had put away six one-litre bottles of beer and was calling for more. Michael and I had long since reached our limit. We persuaded him it would be a good idea to go home and eat. Before we parted he insisted I come round the following day for lunch. He assured me his wife was an excellent cook.

First thing in the morning a young woman turned up with an overnight bag and disappeared into the bedroom. Terry and I went for a joint in the back garden. Ivan didn't indulge; he stayed in his room and studied: he seemed to do little else.

Terry had been maintaining a low profile since Michael's return. He spent most of his time lying on the spare bed in Ivan's room listening to one of the three tapes on the battered cassette player. He had nothing else to occupy him and no money. He asked me about England. He could vaguely remember as a child going shopping with his mother in Glasgow. His father was an engineering student at the time. He also remembers the day they left by boat from Liverpool. He was about five years old. Now all he wanted was to go back, but his father wouldn't hear of it. He thought he could make something of his life over there. He wanted to be a dancer. He took off his shirt and started dancing. He had a good body – spare but well-developed, wide shoulders, flat stomach, long legs – and he moved well. He said that he had danced in a Kano night club a few months ago after winning a competition organized by a television company, but nothing had come of it. He said he knew all the modern dances.

Michael and his girlfriend were up and about when we returned. Michael was sitting on the porch collating exam marks. It seemed a tedious exercise. Terry offered to help. He spent the remainder of the day and a good deal of the evening filling in figures on an endless roll of computer paper.

At lunchtime Michael's girlfriend emerged from the kitchen with bowls of rice. Since I had a lunch date I declined. When I arrived at Ade's bungalow I was told that he had gone out early and had not yet returned. I went back to Michael's place and waited. By three o'clock I was famished and ate; but no sooner had I finished eating than the 'cousin' turned up to say that 'daddy' had still not returned but that I should come and have my food because it was getting late. On the way the 'cousin' asked me about England. He wanted to go to university there when he had finished his first degree. Would I be able to help him?

The meal was a nightmare. A place had been set for me at the head of the table. Ade's wife, well advanced in her pregnancy, waited on me. She had gone to a lot of trouble but I couldn't do any kind of justice to the food, which was a compromise between English and Nigerian cooking: macaroni served with a traditional meat sauce which wasn't too hot, and a separate dish of pepper soup. She could see I wasn't enjoying it but she pretended not to notice. As I struggled with the food we made halting conversation. She said she was from the town of Calabar in the east and didn't much care for Zaria. The people were unfriendly and she was isolated living where they did. All the bungalows on the reserve were owned by the university and rented to university staff. The only time she mixed with the local population was at the market in town, where her inability to speak Hausa meant that she was continually being cheated. Halfway through the meal I had to give up. I smoked a cigarette while she cleared and then I left.

Michael's girlfriend was busy with the housework. She had taken over as the woman of the house: the dishes were washed and stacked; the books were dusted; the sock had been removed from under the settee. It was looking like a proper home. It was easy to see why Michael liked the life. There was a great simplicity in the way social relations were strictly defined. A recent student of his, she was only twenty-two. Her counterpart in England, enjoying an extended adolescence and more concerned with the ideas of sexual equality, would have been much less self-assured. But it was one thing for Michael to say he preferred it; quite another to argue that it was better. We were back again with the idea of Europe's moral bankruptcy: in his own words, that European culture was 'ultimately barren'; that 'having failed to assimilate its technology to its social relations, it had fallen into a trivialized insanity'. Although it was certainly true that I had as much reason to resist this notion as he had to propagate it – I had embraced Europe; he had embraced Africa – it seemed to me he was using this argument to justify what he suspected might be a personal failing: unable to cope with the demands of his own culture, the culture into which had been born, he needed to explain his rejection of it in a way that would make sense. The hidden bonus, of course, was that he was saying precisely what his adopted countrymen wanted to hear. There can hardly be an African intellectual who does not approve of such a settlement. The failure of his marriage to a 'liberated' Englishwoman, the symbol of everything he had found wanting in his own culture, would only have served to confirm his suspicions.

But everything has a price, and the price was his son. Michael may have been fortunate enough to have found a home, but Ivan all-too-painfully lacked an identity. And identity is what it was all about. Ivan's accent alone betrayed him. With his father or with me he spoke in a perfectly normal middle-class British accent; with Terry or with Jimoh he spoke in a perfectly normal Nigerian accent. When confronted with both worlds simultaneously he would often switch accents in mid-sentence. He was neither British nor Nigerian. He was an uneasy hybrid of both.

His confusion revealed itself the night before I left. It had gone midnight. Michael and I had just polished off the last bottle of beer and we were preparing to turn in. Suddenly Ivan came charging out of his room. He was carrying a plastic shopping bag which he dumped on the bonnet of the car.

'He has to go,' he said.

'Who has to go? What are you talking about?' Michael asked.

'He's keeping me awake with his music. How will I be able to work if I can't get to sleep? He has to go.'

'Take it easy,' Michael said.

'I won't, I won't,' he shouted petulantly. 'I want him to go now, this minute. Take him home.'

Michael remained calm. Obviously he had been through something similar before. Terry, wearing only a pair of shorts, leaned against the doorway and said nothing. He knew when to keep quiet.

Ivan was pacing up and down, up and down. He looked as close to exploding as anyone I've seen but he managed to keep a tight lid on it. It might have done him good to have exploded, to have screamed and cursed and rolled on the floor. Then again if he had started he might not have been able to stop. Sometimes these things must be worked out less dramatically.

'Look, Terry will turn the music off, won't you, Terry?'

'He only had to ask,' Terry said. I wasn't deceived by his reasonable tone. There was a mischievous, underhand quality about Terry which I didn't trust. I had little doubt that he had deliberately set about winding Ivan up in order to create a scene to distract him from his boredom. It was Terry, not Ivan, who dictated the terms of their friendship.

86

'Okay, Ivan, why don't you go to bed now? We'll talk about it in the morning,' Michael said.

Ivan had calmed down somewhat. He could see what a fool he was making of himself. But he wasn't quite ready to give in. He had to salvage what was left of his pride.

'But he goes in the morning,' he insisted.

'If that's what you want.'

Abruptly, he started back to his room. Terry moved to let him pass.

'You better take Terry's things back. They shouldn't be left out overnight,' Michael said.

'No, I won't. He's going in the morning.'

Michael sighed.

'I suppose they've just got on top of each other,' I said, after they had both gone.

'I'm worried about him,' Michael said. 'Perhaps he would have been better off in England. I thought I could give him a good life here.'

By the morning Ivan was back to normal, in so far as that was possible. Terry could stay after all. I was leaving for Jos. On the way to the motor-park we called in at Terry's house to collect his mother's address. I had promised to write to her when I got back. The house was filthy. There were children everywhere. Some of them had been sleeping in the living room and had only just got up.

6

'WHERE IS YOUR tax paper?' I was sitting in the front seat
next to the driver. I ignored the elderly man struggling with
the door handle. It was the middle of the morning rush-
hour. Amid the noise and dust a group of officials were
checking for education levy receipts.

'Your tax. Where is your tax?'

'I don't have one,' I said.

'What? What? Why not? Come on, get out.' But however
hard he tried he couldn't open the door. I had no intention
of helping him.

'I'm not a Nigerian citizen, I don't have to pay,' I said. I
turned to the driver: 'Come on, let's go.'

'Wait there,' the old man shouted. 'You get out.'

The driver switched off the engine and threw a piece of
kola-nut into his mouth. I turned back to the official:

'Look, I told you, I'm not a citizen of this country. I've
come from England. I don't have to pay tax.'

'Don't you pay tax in England?'

'Yes.'

'Then where is your paper . . . your receipt?'

'I don't have it with me. I left it in England.' I took out my
passport and showed him my visa. He reached for it but I
held it away from him. I could see him debating whether or
not to press the matter further: after all, I was challenging his

authority. But what I said sounded reasonable. What surprised me was the calm with which my fellow-passengers were taking the delay. Nigerians are a short-tempered, vociferous people. Perhaps they weren't inclined to draw unnecessary attention their way because they themselves didn't possess the required receipts. The longer the old man concentrated his attention on me the more likely it was they would be overlooked. In the meantime I had put away my passport. It was up to him now. He muttered something under his breath and moved to the next vehicle. We were free to go.

Jos lies on a plateau roughly in the centre of the country. As we began climbing, gently at first but more steeply as we approached the city, the air became cooler. It was on this plateau, during excavations in a tin mine in the 1930s, that evidence of a two-thousand-year-old civilization was first discovered in the form of an exceptionally fine terracotta head. The Nok Culture, so called after the village in which the discovery was made, flourished between 900 BC and AD 200 and covered an area approximately 300 miles long and 100 miles wide. It was here that subsequent excavations revealed that the people of Nok knew how to work iron even though many of their tools were stone. The terracotta heads have since become famous; other discoveries included necklaces, bracelets and beads of tin and quartz.

Although we were still in the north, and well within the boundaries of the old Fulani Empire, we were no longer in Hausa country. The two indigenous tribes of this area, the Birom and the Jarawas, are predominantly Christian and speak their own languages. Hausa, however, is used as a lingua franca.

I had intended to spend a few days in Jos but I ended up staying only two nights. My host, the brother of a friend in London, was hospitable enough, but it was obvious from the start, in his manner rather than in anything he said, that he didn't trust me. He knew why I was in the country and this put him on his guard. I can't say that I blamed him. His instincts were sound: writers are not trustworthy. They will use anybody for their own ends.

As we drank beer in his house that evening a friend of his dropped by, a lawyer on his way home from court. He was a short, ugly man in a three-piece pin-stripe suit, patent leather shoes and gold cuff-links. He asked me whether I spoke Yoruba.

'A bit,' I said.

He burst out laughing. 'A bit,' he mimicked. I hadn't realized my English accent was quite so funny, but his aggressive defensiveness, doubtless picked up from my host without anything being said, captured the mood accurately enough. It was then that I decided, churlishly no doubt, that there wasn't much point in staying.

The journey to Lokoja took six hours. On the way we drove through the Federal Capital Territory of Abuja. The need for a new capital city was identified in the mid-1970s, partly in response to the intolerable congestion of Lagos, partly as a drive for a new sense of national unity; as the then Head of State put it: 'The area is not within the control of any of the major ethnic groups in the country. We believe that a new Capital . . . will be for all Nigerians a symbol of their oneness . . .' N10 billion was earmarked for the project. Work began immediately but quickly ran into difficulties as contractors and businessmen siphoned off vast amounts of money into their foreign bank accounts and left the work undone. Apart from the extensive Presidential palace and the international airport, there is little to show in the ten years that have since elapsed. We stopped once for petrol near Abuja and arrived in Lokoja in the middle of the afternoon.

Lokoja is situated on the confluence of the Rivers Niger and Benue. It is here that they meet before turning south to the coast. It was here also, in the middle of the nineteenth century, that a model agricultural farm was established under the auspices of the Society for the Extinction of the Slave Trade and for the Civilization of Africa. The noble aims of this Society were to be achieved through the growth of legitimate trade by providing Africans with the means of producing goods which Britain would purchase, as set out by the then Colonial Secretary, Lord John Russell, in a letter dated 1839:

> . . . it is proposed to establish new commercial relations with those African Chiefs or Powers, within whose dominions the internal Slave-trade of Africa is carried on, and the external Slave-Trade supplied with its victims. To this end, the Queen has directed her Ministers to negotiate conventions or agreements with those Chiefs or Powers; the basis of which conventions would be – First, the abandonment and absolute prohibition of the Slave-trade; and, Secondly, the admission for consumption in this country, on favourable terms, of goods, the produce or manufacture of the territories subject to them. Of those Chiefs, the most considerable rule over the countries adjacent to the Niger and its great tributary streams. It is therefore proposed to despatch an expedition, which would ascend that river by steam-boats, as far as the point at which it receives the Confluence of some of the principal rivers falling into it from the eastward. At these, or at any other stations which may be found more favourable, it is proposed to establish British Factories; in the hope that the Natives may be taught, that there are methods of employing the population more profitable to those to whom they are subject, than that of converting them into slaves, and selling them for exportation to the Slave-traders . . .

The precise nature of African slavery has been the subject of vociferous debate. The majority opinion, among Africans especially, is that internal slavery – that is, Africans enslaved by other Africans – was qualitatively different from European slavery; that Africans treated African slaves better than Europeans treated African slaves, especially in the New World. They point out, in support of their argument, that slaves could, and did, become extremely powerful members of the community. There is some truth in this but it is not the whole truth. Slavery was certainly endemic in large parts of Africa – the Oyo Empire was underpinned by slavery, and its power rested on its ability to control the trade routes between the interior and the coast, between the source of slaves and the European traders on the coast – and there is no reason to suppose that the great numbers of agricultural slaves who fed the towns of Yorubaland were treated any less harshly than the plantation slaves of the *ante-bellum* south. One has only to look at the treatment of servants in present-day Nigeria to get an idea of how harsh the conditions must have been. But the argument doesn't rest on logic or observation. The galling facts of the Atlantic slave-trade and the subsequent colonization of the continent still have the power to whip up a profound anger; and it is part of the emotional climate that is the result of this that dictates that the European be seen as inherently wicked, the African inherently good: if you don't have power on your side then you can comfort yourself with possessing moral superiority. In the process we can put aside the other uncomfortable fact that the Atlantic slave-trade was only possible with the full co-operation of Africans themselves: if, even by the mid-nineteenth century, Europeans couldn't penetrate the continent in search of these slaves, why must we assume they could do so in the seventeenth and eighteenth centuries? The refusal to look at the facts is part of the same impulse which dictates that Africans see Europe as decadent.

At any rate Russell's mission was a failure. One of the

members of the expedition, Samuel Ajayi Crowther, the freed Yoruba slave who was later to become the first African Bishop, records in his journal the catalogue of deaths from malaria: 'Mr Kingdon . . . having died on Tuesday night, was buried this morning'; 'This night a marine, called Cole, died; and Mr Willie, the only officer who had held out longer than the rest, is now very dangerously ill'; 'Mr Willie died last night . . . The Purser's Steward died also a few days later'; 'Capt. B. Allen breathed his last at 10 o'clock this morning . . . Since the death of Capt. B. Allen, to the 7th of November, three officers and a marine have died.' A total of forty-two white men died, all of them unnecessarily. Quinine had already been discovered, but it was only administered to those showing signs of recovery. By the time of the second Expedition, thirteen years later, the use of quinine as a prophylactic had been established, and there was not a single death.

As we pulled into the motor-park I had visions of a boat trip across the water in the early evening as the sun was setting and a leisurely meal on the balcony of a hotel. At first I had difficulty convincing the driver that I wanted to go to the town centre. He seemed anxious that I should carry on to somewhere else. I soon understood why. Lokoja was a glorified village. The mighty Niger, the object of many of the famous names of British exploration – Mungo Park, Denham, Clapperton, the Lander Brothers – was a filthy, sluggish river with a sprinkling of canoes. There wasn't anything even remotely resembling a hotel anywhere in sight. I started back to the motor-park. The laterite road ran alongside the river; on the opposite side, in a continuous line, women sat vacantly behind stalls surrounded by undernourished children. Now and then a group of these children, catching sight of me, would start chanting 'oyinbo, oyinbo, oyinbo.'

Back at the motor-park I was accosted by the driver. He was about to embark on the return journey to Jos.

'What happen?' he asked.

'I want to go to Benin City,' I said.

'No more taxi to Benin. All gone. Why you don't go before when I ask you?' He called a man over. 'Follow him to Okene. From there you get taxi to Benin.'

I had to wait for the taxi to fill up. Presently I was joined by an Asian who had appeared seemingly out of nowhere. He mopped his face with a large white handkerchief and told me that he was a physics teacher from Pakistan serving out a five-year contact. He hated it. He couldn't wait to go back home.

'These people are wery backward, five or six hundred years at least,' he said cheerfully. 'Wery backward. Where are you from?'

'I live in England,' I said evasively.

'Nice place. I went there last year for my cousin's wedding. This place is wery backward. They will never get anywhere.'

The taxi started to fill up.

'Wery backward,' he said.

'I want to get to Benin today,' I said.

'Don't worry, you will get a taxi from Okene. Be patient. One thing I have learnt here is patience. Wery backward.' He settled back in the seat and opened his paper. The driver collected our money. A young girl selling bread came up to me. I shook my head. '*Oyinbo*,' she said and giggled. The driver chased her away with a stick.

It took us an hour to reach Okene. I arrived in time to catch the last taxi to Benin. The only other passenger was a nervous young man who perspired a lot.

'From England?' the driver enquired.

'Yes.'

He fumbled about in the glove compartment and took out a pools coupon.

'Mark it,' he said.

'But I don't know anything about the pools,' I said. He laughed. 'What if you don't win?' I added.

'I will win,' he said. 'Just mark it for me. You people know about pools. That is why they don't allow you to do it.' I couldn't fault his logic. Since the pools come from England, and since they involve English football teams, it followed that I ought to know the secret.

This was a revelation. I put in some crosses at random. He examined what I had marked and nodded.

'You will bring me luck. Thank you.'

We were now back in the tropical rainforest: huge trees on either side of the road bore down on us. The atmosphere was heavy with the humidity and my hands felt clammy. It started raining. Great drops of water hit the body of the car and seeped inside. The windscreen wiper refused to work. The driver had to slow down and operate them manually. We didn't reach Benin until late.

Abraham, my fellow-passenger – 'I am known as A.B. to my friends' – was a Godsend. The only address I had in Benin was of a writer I had never met. It was unlikely I would be able to find him at this hour. In the meantime I was low on money and needed to find somewhere cheap for the night. I explained my problem.

'You must be careful,' A.B. said darkly. 'There are too many loose women in Benin.'

He and the driver entered into a long discussion. They finally settled on a hotel. It was on the other side of the city and in the direction A.B. was going. When we arrived A.B. told me to leave him to do the talking. He explained to the clerk at reception that I was a stranger and that since we were all men together he should give me a reduction. I didn't quite follow the reasoning but I assumed he knew what he was doing. The clerk agreed to a reduction of N5, but at N25 it was still expensive. A.B. pleaded further but the clerk remained adamant. Finally, in disgust, he announced that I would spend the night with him, which is what I had been hoping he would say.

It started raining again. The driver couldn't take us any further along the potholed road that led to A.B.'s aunt's house. In the darkness it was impossible to avoid the puddles. By the time we arrived at the front door my shoes and socks were soaking wet. A young boy with a lantern let us in. A.B.'s cousin was away, so we had the double bed to ourselves. The boy gave us two lengths of cloth. I was exhausted. I was ready to go to sleep but A.B. insisted on telling me about his complicated love-life.

His girlfriend in Benin was a nineteen-year-old student who already had a child by him. He had another girlfriend at the hospital in Okene where he worked as a nurse. He couldn't make up his mind which one he should marry. He had no doubt that they both loved him, proof of which was that each had given him a novel: *Do not go, my love* and *The Secret Lovers*. Because he had been equally impressed with both novels he was now in a quandary. He had to decide which one loved him 'fully'. It was further complicated by the fact that his Benin girlfriend was from a different tribe and therefore considered unsuitable by his parents. I suggested, rather lamely, that perhaps he ought to decide which one *he* loved better. Out of politeness he pretended to take my advice seriously but I could see he thought it beside the point. I was clearly of limited use to him.

First thing in the morning we called at his girlfriend's house. Her father, an elderly man, told him she had gone out. A.B. scowled but said nothing. He went over to some children playing at the far end of the corridor and reached for one of them. The child started crying. He put him down, had a quick word with the father and we left.

'That was my son,' he said, clearly troubled. Presently we

met someone he knew, a woman in her thirties, standing at her front gate cleaning her teeth with a chewing stick. He greeted her, asked after her husband and children, and then wondered whether she knew where his girlfriend had gone.

'I don't like to come all this way and find that she isn't at home so early in the day. I don't like it at all. Please, help me to speak to her when you see her. You can give her good advice,' he said, and added: 'Tell her I will deal with her when I return.' The woman nodded and continued cleaning her teeth. It was difficult to tell what she thought of this outburst. A.B. dabbed at his forehead with his handkerchief. It was a characteristic gesture. He was a rather nervous man who sweated a good deal.

We had gone a little further when A.B. said: 'Why did my son cry when I picked him up? He should be happy to see me.'

On the bus I looked for signs of the old city. Benin, an ancient city-state first reached by a Portuguese explorer in 1486, is one of those vanished empires that have achieved almost mythical status for the glory of its art and the brutality of its customs:

As we neared Benin City we passed several human sacrifices, live women-slaves gagged and pegged on their backs to the ground, the abdominal wall being cut in the form of a cross, and the uninjured gut hanging out. These poor women were allowed to die like this in the sun. Men-slaves, with their hands tied at the back, and feet lashed together, also gagged, were lying about . . . As we neared the city, sacrificed human beings were lying in the path and bush – even in the King's compound the sight and stench of them was awful. Dead and mutilated bodies seemed to be everywhere – by God! may I never see such sights again! . . . In the King's compound, on a raised platform or altar, running the whole breadth of each, beautiful idols were found. All of them were caked over with human blood, and by giving them a slight tap, crusts of blood would, as it were, fly off. Lying about were big bronze heads, dozens in a row, with holes at the top, in which immense carved ivory tusks were fixed . . . The whole place reeked of blood. Fresh blood was dripping off the figures and altars . . .

This is taken from *A Diary of a Surgeon with the Benin Punitive Expedition* in 1897, when the city was sacked and most of it destroyed by fire. The King, Oba Overami, described by another member of the expedition as a 'stout but fine man of considerable intelligence', was banished to the town of Calabar in the east where he died a commoner's death in 1914.

We know only too well the glee with which Europe reacted to yet more evidence of African savagery, justifying as it did the expansionist drive in which Europe was then engaged. But we need not labour the point. It is of no concern to us now. Only the most wilfully bigoted seriously believes any longer in the myth of African savagery. A far more interesting question which Benin does raise is that of the relation between civilization and brutality. It is possible that the Expeditionary Force came across a civilization in decay, one which had produced its finest works at the height of its power and influence in the fifteenth and sixteenth centuries. So impressed were the early Portuguese by the splendour of Benin at this time that the Oba was asked to send an ambassador to Lisbon, and it is claimed that even today a section of the royal palace speaks a language derived from Portuguese which is unintelligible to the ordinary Bini.

But the Punitive Expedition had done its job too well. The ensuing fire, apparently accidental but which nevertheless had left the city 'sweet and pure again', had achieved its aim only by destroying everything. A few crumbling walls here and there – nothing to compare with the ancient walls of Kano – marked the former boundaries. That was all. Benin looked like every other urban centre I had so far seen: corrugated iron and mud huts next to concrete and glass buildings; open gutters; badly tarred roads: if there is such a thing as planning regulations in the major urban centres of the country I was yet to see evidence of it.

We caught a bus to the teaching hospital, where A.B. wanted to apply for a one-year diploma course in psychiatric nursing. A small crowd of young men had gathered outside the admissions' office. The woman in charge had not yet turned up. There was nothing to do but wait. A.B., concerned that I should not be delayed, asked whether he should take me to the university where the writer taught. I told him there was no rush.

The admissions officer finally appeared an hour later. She was a large, middle-aged, extremely vital woman in brightly patterned native dress. She wore gold bracelets on both wrists, a gold necklace, bright red varnish on her nails. The chatter ceased as she strolled past. The clerk hurriedly stood up to greet her. She entered the inner office and closed the door behind her. The hopeful applicants hung around for half-an-hour until one of them finally summoned up the courage to knock. She opened the door and stared at the culprit.

'Yes, what do you want?' The man said something I didn't catch. She surveyed the small crowd.

'Why are there no women here?' she demanded.

Nobody answered.

'Let me tell you here and now that I'm not running this course unless I get some women. Always men, men, men. Go back to your place of work and tell the women to come and apply.'

Nobody moved.

'Didn't you hear me? I said go. I want to see some women before I consider putting on such a course.'

She returned to her office. A.B. wiped his brow and hissed. Someone cracked a feeble joke. We dispersed.

We tracked down the writer's department with difficulty, only to be told that he had travelled the previous day to Lagos. He would be away at least a week. We returned to the hospital. So had everyone else. In Nigeria nothing succeeds like persistence. Progress had been made. Perhaps some bold soul had promised to find a few women. The clerk was busy handing out application forms.

A.B. was now free to 'deal' with his girlfriend. We caught the bus back to her house. Her father was still there. He was sitting on a chair in the corridor playing with the children. He told A.B. that she had returned shortly after we had left and had gone ahead to his parents' house to wait for him. A.B. made fresh overtures to his son. This time the child was more responsive. On our way again he said he was sad that he didn't know the boy better. He would make arrangements to take him back to Okene. He might even take his girlfriend if he was satisfied that she was prepared to 'behave herself properly'.

We had gone a short distance when he pointed to a house where his junior sister lived. A year ago she had argued with the family and run away to live with her boyfriend. The family had immediately disowned her. A.B. had gone to visit her to tell her to go and beg their forgiveness. He had since heard that she had disobeyed him. This showed that she had no respect for him. It betrayed her stupidity: if her husband decided to get rid of her she would be homeless.

Her parents lived on the edge of the city. Many of the bungalows, identical breeze-block buildings, were still in the process of construction. Some of them took years to complete: many consisted of the floor and four walls and nothing else. The lush vegetation, through which narrow footpaths had been fashioned by bare feet, was constantly threatening to claim back the land. Electricity pylons had been erected but there were no wires between them yet.

An old woman with white hair was sitting on the porch. She wore only a wrapper round her waist: she had long passed the age of modesty. She broke into a smile and began clapping. A.B. introduced her as his ninety-two-year-old grandmother. As she didn't speak any English, conversation was impossible, but she never took her eyes off me. He explained that she only rarely saw a white man and that no white man had ever entered her house before.

I was shown into the living room. Like the rest of the house it was unfinished: the walls were unplastered, electricity wires were hanging loose, the concrete floor was rough. It was simply furnished: cheap easy chairs, a table, a calendar on the wall showing Nigeria's leaders since Independence. A woman entered, came over to where I was sitting, and knelt before me. She was A.B.'s sister-in-law, his elder brother's first wife. His brother had met her while he was working in a neighbouring state. Because she was from a different tribe his parents had insisted that he take a second wife from their home village. They had even chosen her for him.

This attitude is the result of Nigeria's multiplicity of tribes, each with its own language and customs, and each insanely suspicious of the others. To move from one village to the next, often a matter of a few kilometres, is to move from one closed world to another. In Bendel State alone, of which Benin is the capital, A.B. counted fourteen separate languages: in Warri they spoke Itsekiri; in Ughell, Urhobo; in Kwale, Kwale; in Asaba, Bendel-Ibo; in Benin, Edo; in Bomadi and Burutu, Ijaw; in Uromi and Ubiaja, Ishan; in Igarra, Igarra; in Ososo, Ososo; in Ibillo, Okpameri; in Afuze, Ona; in Auchi, Auchi; in Osoko, Osoko; in Agbor,

Ika. Of course, it is absurd that a woman from Warri who marries a man from Asaba should be shunned as a foreigner. Both of them belong to a wider and much more powerful geographic entity known as Nigeria. It occurred to me that such people, albeit in the majority, are not merely anachronisms but are powerless. The future of the country hardly rests with them. The world they inhabit is too small. What they think and feel is important only to them; they can say nothing for the country as a whole. They are conservative, backward, even reactionary; they are peasants who are required only to produce food for the cities where those who make the real decisions – artists, bankers, businessmen, lawyers, engineers, doctors and civil servants – live and work. And this view, however unfashionable, seems to me the only tenable one. It is even possible that many of these small languages will eventually die out. There is nothing tragic about this. There is no virtue in hanging on to so-called 'cultural artefacts' for their own sake. Those who argue otherwise do so out of misguided romanticism and at the expense of the country's political viability which simply cannot support the existence of so many differing allegiances. It is perfectly possible that only the three major languages will remain – Hausa, Yoruba and Igbo – each of which is spoken by upwards of twenty million people. These are the languages in which the indigenous literatures will be created, the only languages which can support such literatures, though there are a few others which are spoken by sufficient numbers to survive: Efik, Fulani, Ibibio, Nupe, Tiv and Urhobo.

A.B.'s family were preparing to travel to their village, sixty kilometres away, to harvest their crops. His brother had gone to collect the truck which would take them there. They would be gone four days. A.B. meanwhile excused himself to go in search of his girlfriend. His grandmother, who was also going to the farm, stood in the doorway and stared at me. A peasant who thought I was a white man, she also credited me with magical powers.

A.B. had already told me about my magical powers. He had said: 'We believe you people are witches. How else could you make planes that fly in the sky?' But he had added: 'We blacks are also witches. We use our witchcraft for destruction whereas you use yours for your comfort.' There was a certain logic in what he said, rooted as it was in the evidence of an impressive technology. It went a long way to explain why I attracted so much attention. It wasn't simply that I was an unusual sight; what made me even more unusual was that I was walking along the road instead of being driven around in an air-conditioned car. When I pointed out that knowledge of this technology was available to everyone, that Britain was full of Nigerians studying every conceivable subject under the sun, he came out with an even more extraordinary statement. Although he admitted that black men overseas were taught the white man's magic, it was also the case that after they had acquired this knowledge they were forbidden to return home. They were given all manner of incentives to stay – house, car, job, wife – but if they still insisted on returning they were killed. When I told him that this was simply untrue he smiled. What else would I say?

A.B. called me to come out the back, where he was sitting with his girlfriend in front of the open kitchen. The cooking was done over an open fire: a semi-circle of blackened stones lay in a small heap on the bare earth in the middle of the makeshift structure – three sides of corrugated tin, thatched roof – next to a blackened pot.

A tall, flat-chested woman in a short skirt and cotton blouse, she was looking appropriately subdued having presumably been 'dealt with' by A.B. I was later to hear him say, during a short and angry exchange: 'I am a man, I can deal with you; you are a woman, you can't deal with me.' He asked me if I wanted to bathe, and then instructed her to go and fetch a bucket of rain water from the well in front of the house. He directed me to the bathroom nearby, a square, doorless cement structure four feet high with a slimy floor and a hole in the corner for the waste. Afterwards I changed into fresh clothes, said goodbye to his grandmother, and we went out.

A.B. was anxious to find me a 'respectable' hotel for the night, one that didn't encourage prostitutes. He himself was uncertain where he would sleep but he wanted to get me settled first. He knew of a place not too far away where he thought the price might be reasonable. His girlfriend walked in front of us with my bag. It was heavy with the books I had bought since I had left Lagos. She wouldn't hear of me taking it from her.

By now I was used to the children shouting *oyinbo* whenever they saw me coming. But it was also beginning to irritate me. Once I surprised them by lunging at them and shouting that I was going to do my magic on them if they didn't shut up. This amused A.B. and terrified the children, who fled in hysterics to the safety of their mothers. A.B. pointed out a hotel owned by a Nigerian woman with the unlikely name of Anna Smith. She had married an English-man many years ago and had been left it by him when he had finally returned home. He also pointed to an abandoned building, only half-completed, which was the object of a long-standing feud between two men, one rich, the other poor, over the rightful ownership. Neither dared complete the work: the rich man threatened litigation; the poor man threatened witchcraft. Belief in witchcraft allows for a certain measure of democracy in human affairs.

I insisted that we stop at a drinking parlour. I was thirsty from the walk and wanted a cold drink. A.B. hesitated and then only reluctantly agreed. Inside there was a group of rowdy young men who calmed down the moment we entered. I wondered whether I had made a mistake. I had been warned often enough of unemployed thugs who think nothing of sticking a knife in a man for the small change, which is why I kept most of my money in my socks. I couldn't have been further from the truth. A.B. told me later that one of them had remonstrated with the others to behave in front of me so as not to create a bad impression.

It was irksome to be treated as an outsider in my father's country. It happened again later in the evening while we were having a meal. A wrestling match was in progress on the television and the customers were being noisily partisan. They became quite subdued the moment I entered. Try as I might I simply wasn't going to be allowed to disappear into the background. Invisibility was a luxury I wasn't going to be permitted; it was a luxury I had never been permitted. I have never been able to understand the discomfort of the Trinidadian writer, V. S. Naipaul, at being treated like a native during his visit to India. In *An Area of Darkness*, the book which came out of the visit, he writes:

> And for the first time in my life I was one of the crowd. There was nothing in my experience to distinguish me from the crowd eternally hurrying into Churchgate Station. In Trinidad to be an Indian was to be distinctive. To be anything there was distinctive; difference was each man's attribute. To be Indian in England was distinctive; in Egypt it was more so. Now in Bombay I entered a shop or a restaurant and awaited a special quality of response. And there was nothing. It was like being denied part of my reality. Again and again I was caught. I was faceless. I might sink without a trace into that Indian crowd.

It sounded enviable to me; but perhaps if I did make it to Egypt or Brazil, two places where I was assured most people looked just like me, I would feel just as disoriented. And I had to admit that despite my present irritation I also derived a perverse pleasure from being singled out from the mass.

And yet the matter wasn't as simple as that. If I was treated as an outsider among people who didn't know me, I was treated as family by those who did. The ambiguity of my position generated a corresponding ambiguity in my responses: was I Nigerian or wasn't I; if so, to what degree? We long for simplicity but are constantly denied it.

In the meantime I was weary and I opted for an early night. A.B. escorted me back to the hotel, made sure I was comfortable, and then announced that he was going to try and persuade his girlfriend's father to let him sleep there. I gave him full marks for audacity.

A.B. came round early in the morning with breakfast: a flask of Bournvita, a loaf of bread, a boiled egg, a tin of condensed milk, some cubes of sugar wrapped up in a page from an exercise book. It was thoughtful of him and I appreciated it.

As I ate I could see that he was tremendously excited. I had hardly finished when he showed me an adage he had come across in one of the daily papers. It was in a regular column headed Positive Thinking. It said: 'Nothing ventured, nothing gained. Be willing to risk failure in order to succeed.' He read it twice and shook his head in admiration, then tore it out carefully and put it in his shirt pocket. He confided his ambition to go to India or America to study medicine. He didn't think he would try Britain where, he said, 'the standards are too high'. He wanted my advice as a man who knew something of the world. I didn't quite know what to say, except to list the practical difficulties: Did he have the necessary qualifications? How would he finance himself? Did he realize how stiff the competition was likely to be? But I couldn't dampen his optimism and I didn't want to. If I had listened to everybody's advice I wouldn't have

sitting in that room talking to him and planning to
e this book. He said he didn't mind how long it took
or what he had to do while he was studying. The point
s to become a doctor and therefore a big man. Any price
was worth it; any amount of suffering could be borne. I
knew he meant every word of it. There is little the average
Nigerian won't do to advance himself; there are few who
don't know the score. It is the scale of their ambition that
will one day make the country great.

But I did point out that if he really believed what he had
said the day before he would never be able to return home.
He hadn't thought that far. All he knew was that the white
man's magic, Indian magic particularly, was extremely
potent. That was why he personally only ever went to
Indian doctors, and why hospitals with Indian staff did
better business than hospitals with African staff. Not that
the people had much faith in doctors to begin with. In the
area where he worked it was difficult to get anyone to attend
the hospital, consequently many of them died unnecessarily
from hernia, 'frequent stooling', and goitre. When a person
dies the community consults a medium, since somebody
has to be responsible. The usual method was to take nail
parings from the deceased and suspend them in a cloth over
a bowl of water. The medium is then, by some mysterious
process, presented with a name, whereupon the guilty party
is charged. If he refuses to confess he is beaten until he does
so. It sounded to me like a foolproof method of establishing
guilt. This is the kind of practice over which European
anthropologists begin drooling at the mouth. This is Africa,
the real Africa, the Africa of superstition and ignorance and
'traditional' belief; the pure Africa uncontaminated by
Western science. Its exoticism is undeniable. It is about as
exotic as a bunch of Mississippi swamp dwellers who believe
in worshipping rattle-snakes. No one would suggest that
this was the real America, pure and uncontaminated, merely

an aberration. It is what happens to a community when it is divorced from the mainstream of modern life; when it has become, for whatever reason, isolated from current ideas about the nature of the world.

I changed the subject. Out of curiosity, and considering the way he was treating his girlfriend, I asked him whether he didn't think that the position of women in Nigeria left a lot to be desired. It was a leading question, of course, but he didn't make the connection. He agreed with me, and then described how women were treated in the community where he worked. Because of the drift to the cities by the men there was a surplus of women. It wasn't unusual for one man to have up to five wives, each of whom was forced into competition with the others for her husband's attentions. This made the men lazy, men who, by remaining behind in the first place, had already demonstrated their lack of initiative. These men were content to leave their wives to fend for themselves and their children while they spent all day drinking and chasing other women. He personally thought such behaviour despicable. It happened that at the time there was an International Women's Conference in Nairobi. The report in the paper he had with him referred to a motion that had been passed calling on women to go on strike. What did he think of that? He laughed. No Nigerian woman will ever go on strike. If she does her husband will simply throw her out and tell her to go and fend for herself. I pointed out that, according to him, the women already appeared to be doing just this, but he merely shrugged. He was a man of contradictions. It was pointless pressing him.

It appeared that A.B. already considered himself something of a doctor. He told me that he had purchased some anti-malaria vaccines and a packet of disposable injections and that he was considering a trip to his village to set up an impromptu clinic. Apparently he made money this way fairly regularly. Malaria was endemic in the villages and the people had more faith in injections than in drugs. He also said that he carried out abortions, as did many of his fellow-nurses, but this was dangerous because the penalty if you were caught was imprisonment. I asked him how much he charged. He said that depended on the stage of the pregnancy: anywhere between N60 and N120.

On the way out we collected his girlfriend. As before, she carried my bag and walked ahead of us. When we got to his house his grandmother still insisted on regarding me as a visitor from another planet, which is what I suppose I was in her eyes: as far as she was concerned Europe may have been Venus for all she knew. There was a truck outside the house and an immense amount of activity inside. I was introduced to his older brother, a short, balding man in his thirties.

Once again I was deposited in the living room and left to gaze at the bare walls. It was then that I decided to return to Lagos. I was tired of travelling. I could get my visa extended and relax for a few days before heading east on the second leg of my journey, which is what I had planned all along.

From somewhere in the house a child screamed. I went to investigate. I found A.B. in his brother's room. His sister-in-law, the woman I had met the previous day, was holding a child on her lap. A.B. was standing by the window trying to get the top off one of the vials of anti-malaria serum. The vial broke in his hand and the liquid spilt down the front of his shirt. He cursed and reached for another. The sweat was pouring down his face as he attacked the top of the second vial with a kitchen knife. A disposable syringe lay on the table. It had evidently been used on the other children but he wasn't about to discard it just yet. This time he was successful. The budding doctor – M.D. pending – filled the syringe, squirted a little out in a deft, professional manner, and then plunged the needle into the child's backside. He scowled as he emptied the contents in a swift movement and then ordered the eldest child present to clear up after him. His sister-in-law thanked him and then asked whether he had any tablets for her stomach, which wasn't feeling right and had kept her awake all night.

'Don't you know these things cost money?' he snapped; then, to me: 'These people think I get it free because I'm a nurse. This is what I wanted to take to my village. Look what I've wasted.' He packed what was left into his bag. 'I'm going to charge you for all this,' he added. As he got up to go she thanked him. He didn't bother to acknowledge her. He was unhappy about the way he had been manoeuvred into wasting some of his precious medicine, which represented part of his capital investment. And he knew that his threat was an idle one: she was family after all, and besides she didn't have any money to give.

His brother came in to say goodbye. They were ready to go to the farm. He gave me a cassette tape:

'I hope you wouldn't mind accepting this,' he said. 'It is our native music to remind you of your visit to Benin City. Perhaps one day you will come with us to the farm and eat bush meat and see how we live there.' Touched, I thanked him.

7

Two DAYS AFTER I arrived back in Lagos there was a coup. Akin woke me up at six in the morning with the news. His older brother had been the first to hear about it and had come over to alert us. He and Shade were listening to martial music on the radio. I thought of my wife and friends in England. Just before I had left I had said to them, only half-jokingly, that a coup would be good for the book; but when we drove out, later in the day, the city was calm. There were more military roadblocks and we got stopped more often. The exchange would go something like this:

'What is your name?'

'Akin Williams.'

'Who are you?'

'I'm a lawyer.'

A short silence, then:

'Who is your friend?'

'My name is Adewale Pearce.'

'What is your work?'

'I'm a teacher.' I said teacher because it was simpler, and in any case to have called myself a writer might have been to invite trouble: writer would imply journalist, and journalists, particularly foreign-looking ones, are not encouraged by military regimes.

The coup had been a strictly military affair. The Head of

State, Major-General Muhammadu Buhari, had simply been replaced by Major-General Ibrahim Babangida, a member of Buhari's Supreme Military Council, now re-named the Armed Forces Ruling Council. In the new regime's radio broadcast, transmitted every fifteen minutes, they spoke of Buhari's failure to solve the country's economic problems, and the way in which 'a select few members' of the Supreme Military Council had arrogated to themselves 'absolute knowledge of problems and solutions', ignoring in the process advice from their colleagues and from the country at large. To demonstrate their goodwill they repealed Decree 4 'with immediate effect'. They also promised to settle the question of the IMF loan, which had been dragging on for over a year.

Akin was sceptical. Later that evening, unable to go out because of the dusk-to-dawn curfew, we sat in his office and discussed the recent development. He said: 'If you hear that two soldiers are arguing you can be sure it's about chopping.' To 'chop' means to eat, both literally and metaphorically; in other words, one of them is unhappy about the division of the spoils. This is Nigeria all over, but entirely justified in the context of the country's political scene since independence. This was the fifth successful coup in twenty-five years. No one had any reason to suppose that the new regime would be any better than the others. All it did was underline the nation's chronic instability; it also underlined the helplessness of individual Nigerians to determine their leadership. Nobody could oppose the army, an army which was more concerned with turning itself into an internal political weapon than a buffer against foreign aggression.

And yet, as even Akin pointed out, the army was far and away the most disciplined force in the country, an observation which must be immediately qualified. Consider the following. A perfectly ordinary citizen is walking along the road. Turning a corner he inadvertently bumps into a soldier. The man, his profuse apologies notwithstanding, is immediately pushed up against the wall by the soldier and his colleagues, all of them privates. Another man, middle-aged, smartly dressed, obviously well-to-do, has observed the whole incident from his car. He hurries over to plead with the soldiers. He, too, is pushed up against the wall, and then the pair of them are hauled off to the nearby barracks. An officer is on duty. He listens in silence to his subordinates, promises to deal with the two offenders, and dismisses them. When the soldiers are out of earshot he apologizes to the two men. He explains that there is nothing he can do: even though he is an officer he cannot afford to offend even a common private. It is too risky.

Such stories can be multiplied forever. Everyone has witnessed similar scenes, and yet Akin can still call the army disciplined. This is because he has in mind two failed civilian administrations. The first, from 1960 to 1966, and the second, from 1979 to 1984, had both proved themselves incapable of managing the nation's affairs with any degree of probity. In this respect it was the Second Republic, under President Shehu Shagari, which demonstrated the depths to which Nigeria's leaders were prepared to descend in their desire to enrich themselves at the country's expense. Entering office with foreign reserves put at between N2.6 and N5.6 billion, and earning, in their period of office, an estimated N43 billion from petroleum sales, they left the country with an external debt of N12.9 billion. The scale of the corruption left even Nigerians open-mouthed. Overnight, senators became millionaires by inflating government contracts and pocketing the difference, by awarding import licences to the highest bidder, by stealing government property and selling it on the open market. The country was engulfed in a madness that inevitably seeped downwards as everyone tried to get in on the act.

The sudden leap in the price of oil is the obvious scapegoat. In 1970 oil sales amounted to N200 million; in 1974/75, following the oil price rises, the figure was N2,500 million. The then Head of State, General Gowon, declared that for Nigeria 'money is no longer a problem'. The Polish journalist Ryszard Kapuscinski, in his study of the downfall of the Shah of Iran, *Shah of Shahs*, has charted the psychology of the oil boom:

> Oil kindles extraordinary emotions and hopes, since oil is above all a great temptation. It is the temptation of ease, wealth, strength, future, power ... Oil creates the illusion of a completely changed life, life without work, life for free. Oil is a source that anaesthetizes thought, blurs vision, corrupts ...

This is certainly true in Nigeria's case. It is why Nigerians, at least those who had access to all this oil money, those who travelled abroad and stayed only in the best hotels, ate only the most expensive meals, bought only the most expensive cars, developed an arrogance that made them notorious in most of the world's capitals. They chopped, as Akin put it, and they chopped well. They were the ten-per-cent men, the so-called comprador capitalists, men who were content to act as agents for foreign companies to the detriment of indigenous industries. We are talking in terms of millions. The most celebrated case involved the director of the National Youth Service Corps and his deputy who, for services rendered to foreign contractors and suppliers, accumulated N20 million in their two years of office.

But oil alone was not responsible: oil merely provided the means for greater corruption. We have to look further for the cause, which lies in an attitude of mind. Consider the following:

> If by the time I was forty years old, I had not acquired the requisite funds to proceed to the U.K. to study law, I would settle permanently to a business career. That was

my grand strategy, and the tactics I adopted was to launch a five-year plan for myself beginning with 6 March 1943, my thirty-fourth birthday . . . In that time I was going 'to make myself formidable intellectually', 'morally invulnerable', 'to make all the money that it is possible for a man of my brains and brawn to make in Nigeria', and 'to acquire a profession'. 'After getting this profession,' I added, and as it turned out, prophetically, 'I should like to make more money.'

Again:

First, that, henceforth, I shall dedicate my life to the emancipation of the continent of Africa from the shackles of imperialism, and to the redemption of my country from the manacles of foreign rule.

Secondly, that in order to earn an honest livelihood, henceforth, I shall devote my energies either to work on my own or to work for others, with the sole aim of accumulating wealth to ensure that I shall never be in want.

Thirdly, that, henceforth, I shall utilize my earned income to secure my enjoyment of a high standard of living and also to give a helping hand to the needy.

This first is taken from the autobiography of Chief Obafemi Awolowo, the country's first Leader of the Opposition; the second from the autobiography of Nnamdi Azikiwe, the country's first President when Nigeria was declared a republic in 1963. With such men at the helm one might be forgiven for thinking of politics in Nigeria as a business proposition. It is difficult indeed to find one prominent Nigerian leader who betrays anything approaching political thought.

There was one exception. His name was General Murtala Muhammad. He seized power in July 1975 to clean up the country. In his address to the nation he stated: 'Fellow

Countrymen, the task ahead of us calls for sacrifice and self-discipline at all levels of our society. This government will not tolerate indiscipline. This government will not condone abuse of office.' For the first and only time in the nation's brief history civil servants were found 'on seat' at seven-thirty in the morning. Seven months later he was assassinated in an unsuccessful coup. Today he is remembered as a great man. The international airport at Lagos is named after him.

The post-oil madness produced a fresh outburst of literary creativity by a younger generation of Nigerian writers appalled by the moral collapse of Nigerian society. Festus Iyayi's *Violence*, published in 1979, is a long, sprawling, undisciplined novel which derives its power from the author's outrage at the injustices of a system which reduces human beings to chattel and love to a commodity whose value is measured in naira and kobo.

The theme of the novel is the prostitution of women in Nigerian society. It contrasts the lives of two couples: Idemudia and his wife, Adisa, who are poor; Queen and her husband, Obofun, who are wealthy. One day, driving through a slum in Lagos looking for cheap labour, Obofun stops beside Idemudia and asks him if he would like a job unloading cement at his wife's hotel. Idemudia, unemployed and on the verge of starvation, jumps at the opportunity, and so begins a relationship between the two couples who symbolize either end of the social scale which is permitted to co-exist in the same city and which, having the fact of money in common – the lack of it on the one hand, the abundance of it on the other – dictates a base level of sexual morality which flatters neither.

For Queen it is a deliberate choice. She has got where she is by hardening her heart and opening her legs to any man who can help her make money. There is no tenderness in her: she is vicious, greedy and utterly mercenary. When, for instance, she needs a large consignment of milk and eggs for the hotel, she simply gets in touch with the relevant civil servant and sleeps with him. She feels nothing for him, she even finds him repellent; and when she has fulfilled her side of the bargain she drops him without a moment's hesitation and turns her attention to her next challenge.

Queen's obsession with money, and the method she uses to get it, has its own price. By killing everything that is good in her she also destroys her sense of responsibility towards her family. She has become indifferent not only to the men she jumps into bed with but to her only daughter. This indifference is the direct cause of the girl's rape in the sitting room of the hotel at the same moment as she is bedding the civil servant. The juxtaposition of the two events is, of course, significant in terms of the novel: it is a statement about the inadequacy of money to make good the absence of love.

Adisa is the antithesis of Queen in every respect except beauty. But to be a beautiful woman, and poor, is a dubious blessing in Nigerian society. Her integrity is not in doubt. When she finally submits to Obofun's demands, it is only because she can see no other way out of her predicament. It happens that on the day Idemudia works for Queen unloading cement it is raining heavily and he catches a chill. His condition deteriorates until he is forced into hospital. The pitiful amount of money he has earned is soon dissipated on drugs, and Adisa is left to fend for herself. Obofun, who had spied her from the car on the day he picked up her husband, offers her money in return for sex. His motives aren't simply the desire to bed a beautiful woman. If he is a little more human than his wife his humanity resides in the knowledge that people like him are contaminated, and in attempting to sublimate his feelings of self-disgust he needs to contaminate others. When he finally manages to get his way, in yet another hotel he and his wife own, and in which Adisa submits to him without encouragement or pleasure – 'She struggled once more and attempted to break free but it was no use. Obofun weighed down heavily on her and her fight was nothing but the last spasmodic movements of a dying animal' – he is suddenly filled with remorse. Adisa, it would seem, ultimately has more power over him than he has over her: the power of forgiveness.

It is in the nature of things that Idemudia learns of his wife's betrayal. It happens in a curious way. Idemudia, fully recovered, is employed by Queen on one of her building sites. Her contract has almost expired but she is finding it difficult to hurry the job along because her workers are dissatisfied with their conditions and are talking of a strike. Ordinarily she would simply dismiss them on the spot and hire a new batch from the vast reservoir of the city's unemployed, but to do so would mean slowing down further the rate of progress. It transpires that Idemuria, one of her best workers, is also the most vocal. Too mean to simply raise their wages, she attempts to buy him off. It doesn't occur to her that he might refuse. She merely assumes that everyone, like her, has a price. It is indicative of the narrowness of the world she inhabits that his refusal stuns her. But she is nothing if not tenacious, and when she has recovered from the shock she summons him and attempts to seduce him. He turns her down. This is more than she can bear. She tells him of his wife's infidelity.

The best novel to come out of this shameful period of Nigerian history is Ben Okri's *The Landscapes Within* (1981). The central motif of the book is the mutilated body of a girl on the beach in Lagos which the hero, Omovo, and a friend accidentally stumble upon:

They lit a match and covered the flickering flame with two cupped hands. It was a girl alright. She had been mutilated. Her hair had been roughly shaved. The eyes were half-open. Her mouth pouted so that a small area of her white teeth gleamed. Her flowered cotton dress had been terribly ripped and was bloodstained. A white, strangely-smelling cloth had been used to cover her lower parts. She had no shoes on. There was a small bronze cross round her neck that dangled towards the earth. She was a pretty girl no more than ten years old. There was a look on her face. Totally unfathomable in its blank expression.

This image haunts the novel and is returned to again and again. This image, with its dark overtones of sinister practices, is the dominant symbol of the depths to which the society has plunged.

Omovo is a painter. He paints what he sees, which is filth and squalor and decay. One of his paintings, of a 'large greenish scum' near his house, is hung at an important exhibition to which a sprinkling of prominent Lagos citizens have been invited. The painting does not please the assembled socialites. They want to be flattered, not re-minded of the corruption they themselves have deliberately created in order to maintain their scandalous standard of living. Nor do they care for art. They are philistines, and that in a country with ancient and powerful artistic tradi-tions. To cover up their uneasiness they gather round the picture and snigger amongst themselves.

Between the inherited tradition and the contemporary reality the Nigerian artist might be forgiven for sinking into despair, an emotion which Omovo comes perilously close to embracing in the course of the novel and which he transcends only at the price of great personal suffering. Others aren't so fortunate, or so courageous. In a society that seeks to destroy everything that is pure many perish. Such is the case with Omovo's girlfriend, seventeen years old and already married off to a man she loathes.

Within their narrow, isolated community, theirs is the only relationship uncontaminated by the squalor around them. But the forces which are in control of the society are far stronger than the love they nurture for each other. Such purity cannot be allowed to flourish in the prevailing cesspool. It is even denied consummation. They are frustrated at every turn by the unceasing vigilance of her jealous husband. In the end she flees back to her village and is accidentally murdered by a member of the neighbouring village, the victim of a long-standing feud between the two communities. Like the girl on the beach, she is a sacrifice.

The moral outrage of these writers, who are part of a genuine movement by a younger generation of Nigerian intellectuals, seems to me significant and the key to the country's future. For the first time Nigerians themselves are holding those in positions of power accountable for their actions. We are also beginning to see the emergence of a truly indigenous intellectual class, a class which takes its responsibilities seriously; that of criticizing society's failings without recourse to the tired rhetoric of anti-colonialism. Anti-colonial rhetoric can never amount to an intellectual position because it is defined in terms of negatives and its appeal is largely emotional.

Because of the coup I decided to delay my departure for the east. However peaceful things might seem now there was always the possibility of further trouble. If that happened Lagos was the best place to be. I was thinking more in terms of my career than my safety; it isn't every day that one happens to be around when there is a coup. I borrowed a typewriter and wrote an article. Although the airports were closed and the borders sealed I could have it ready to send to England by courier with the first flight out. My wife would know what to do. It didn't work out like that. I discovered later that the newspaper I had in mind sent out one of their regular journalists as soon as they could. I met this man – English, white – quite by chance after I returned to England. He said: 'I only have to spend twenty-four hours in a country to know what's going on. I don't even have to leave the airport.' It is this attitude which infuriates so many Africans, and it is the reason why Africa is so consistently misrepresented in the European media. He wouldn't have spoken that way about Poland or the United States. But Africa is different; Africa is simple.

The reports in the British press immediately after the coup talk exclusively about the ousted regime's inability to solve the growing economic crisis, the result of falling oil revenue. They also refer to its refusal to submit to the International Monetary Fund's demands – devaluation of the naira, liberalization of imports, the removal of petroleum subsidies – in order to qualify for a loan. This is only half the truth. As the subsequent debate in the Nigerian newspapers demonstrated, Nigerians were uneasy about the loan, particularly after the British Foreign Secretary rushed to Lagos to notify the new Head of State that should Nigeria refuse the loan she wouldn't be able to count on her 'friends' for support. Support for what? You don't have to be an economist to understand that import liberalization could only be to the advantage of Europe who needs the huge market that Nigeria represents to solve her own unemployment problem. It certainly wouldn't help Nigerians, who would be forced to buy cheaper European goods to the further detriment of indigenous industry. The comprador capitalists would come out on top once again. In the meantime the ordinary Nigerian would suffer.

If Buhari's regime had become unpopular the reason lies elsewhere. Akin had said to me: 'Personally I don't mind suffering if it's for the good of the country; but I'm damned if I'm going to suffer while others are chopping.' Three events associated with the Buhari regime stand out, all of them concerned with the WAI campaign.

One month after the launch of the first phase of the campaign, 'Queue Culture', a brigadier in the army walked into the external affairs and armed forces section of the Federal Inland Revenue in Lagos to secure a tax clearance certificate. He was told to join the queue. He refused and demanded to see the most senior officer on duty. When he was again refused he drew his gun and threatened to deal 'ruthlessly' with the officer. He was given his certificate.

Then there was the story of the 53 suitcases. That same April the government announced a change in the colours of the currency to render useless the N5 million believed to be illegally circulating abroad. All entry points were closed for three days with the exception of the international airport in Lagos, and everyone entering the country was to be thoroughly searched. In the middle of the exercise the former ambassador to Saudi Arabia flew in with 53 suitcases. He was met at customs by a high-ranking army officer and despite the tight security he was not searched. The Nigerian press, ever on the look-out, went to town. It transpired that the former ambassador's protector was no less a person than the aide-de-camp to the Head of State.

The final incident occurred in a hotel suite in Vienna the following May. A certain Alhaji Abubakar Alhaji, head of the OPEC delegation meeting in the Austrian capital, was robbed of £17,000. Challenged by the Nigerian press, he claimed that he had only just taken the money out of his bank account in England, in line with the government directive to all public officers to close their foreign accounts. This was Decree 1: 'A public officer shall not maintain or operate a bank account in any country outside Nigeria.' But how did he come to have so much money in the first place? And why hadn't he immediately changed it into naira, as stipulated? So far, not so good. What was the government going to do about it? Three months later nothing had happened; six months later Alhaji Abubakar Alhaji was appointed head of the Ministry of National Planning. And then the ever-vigilant Nigerian press began to unearth some interesting facts, chief of which was that this same Alhaji was related to the Head of State by marriage.

Examples of corruption and nepotism, like examples of indiscipline, can be multiplied *ad nauseam*. The point is this: while the great mass of the Nigerian people welcomed the WAI exercise as long overdue, and were quite willing to pay the necessary price if it meant the restoration of civil order, they were not prepared to subsidize their leaders in the process.

The suggestion that there might be a counter-coup came from Segun, a doctor. He was one of those excitable men with an exaggerated sense of dramatic possibilities. He was fond of giving the impression that he was privy to inside information through his many contacts. He had rushed over on the morning of the coup to inform us that this was only the beginning, and by the time he was through the country had been plunged into civil war. That was why he was planning to go to America for further studies, 'until things cool down'.

I had met Segun a few weeks earlier, when I had first arrived in Lagos. He and Akin were friends from university, where they had shared a room. He had said: 'Pearce, don't you remember me? St Saviour's. We used to pluck mangoes from the tree in the school compound.' I remembered the school, I remembered plucking mangoes, I didn't remember Segun.

I was beginning to discover how much I had forgotten. Whenever Akin and I reminisced about school days he would casually mention a name I had until that moment completely forgotten. One Saturday afternoon I got him to drive me to the house in which I had grown up. It was only when I saw it again that I realized how privileged my childhood had been. In this suburb of the city the roads were paved and every house stood in its own grounds. Our house overlooked the lagoon. It was here that my brothers and I used to spend hours searching the water for jellyfish to melt in the sun. It was in the lagoon that I saw my first corpse, the bloated body and straw-like hair of a young woman floating gently along with the current. I had nightmares for a week afterwards. I was being chased by a mummy in a dark, empty house. I would have liked to have gone into the compound, even look over the house, but the moment I stepped out of the car I was challenged by a policeman. He wanted to know my business. I was about to explain but thought better of it. Nigerians are not a sentimental people.

As the days passed and it became clear that Segun was wrong, that there would be no counter-coup – let alone a civil war – I began to think of going east. But I kept putting it off from one day to the next. It was only after I returned to England that I was able to identify this period as the beginning of a depression. Seeing the house again after all these years had affected me in a way I would never have suspected. It led me to thinking about the breakdown of my parents' marriage, which was itself the symbol of the larger problem of the conflict of cultures: as the product of that marriage I *was* the conflict. I had thought, once, foolishly, that it could be resolved by an act of will, but there are some things for which there is no resolution and in which the will can only be treacherous. I owed allegiance to both – both parents, both cultures – and it was impossible to act without betraying one or other of them. It began with the question of where I lived. Nobody can live in two countries at the same time. I had chosen to live in England – I even had an English wife – but where did this leave Nigeria?

The real irony is that by treating me so well Akin only compounded the problem. And not only Akin. His entire family took their cue from him. One evening his sister treated me to a meal at a seaside restaurant owned by a friend of hers. The restaurant was popular with the expatriates who worked in the nearby embassies. She introduced me as 'our cousin from England'. I was tremendously touched, of course. Who wouldn't have been? But I also resented the impossible demands they were making on me. By drawing me in so completely, by making me part of the family, they were telling me that I had a place here. They were also telling me I had responsibilities.

On another occasion Akin and I went to visit a friend of his. We drank steadily and by midnight found ourselves discussing the state of the country. The conversation hinged on whether or not Nigerians were capable of running their own affairs. The friend gave the example of a certain hotel which had gone to pieces ever since it had been taken over by a Nigerian. Under its previous, foreign management it had been a pleasant place to stay; now it was a wreck: the staff were rude, the food was appalling, the rooms were filthy. He predicted that the same would happen to the recently completed Sheraton Hotel in Lagos. I said: 'That's a terrible thing to have to say.' I was as saddened as he was by his comment because I knew it to be true. It is difficult to find even one person in the country who takes a pride in doing a job of work properly, who isn't interested only in the money. This includes, as we have seen, people at the top. It means, for one thing, that young people have no models to emulate, which is why corruption is a difficult cycle to break; for another, it means that whatever one's personal feelings one must participate in the corruption in order to get anything done. But Akin's friend immediately went on the defensive. He said: 'That doesn't mean we should keep on employing you people.' He had let himself go sufficiently to criticize his country in front of a foreigner, and now he felt he had to put me firmly in my place. Akin said, quietly: 'You don't have to talk to him like that. His father was a Nigerian. He's one of us.'

I also envied what I saw as the relative simplicity of Akin's life. It made mine seem fragmented in comparison. Against the security of family and place, both of which he could take absolutely for granted, his life followed a pre-ordained pattern: school, university, job, marriage, children. This isn't to suggest that his life was easy. He worked hard for what he had and he fulfilled the many obligations that were the price of it. If his wife's uncle turned up at midnight and chose to stay until three in the morning drinking beer there was nothing he could do about it. His personal feelings about the man were irrelevant. He was required only to show the proper respect. He, in his turn, would demand the same. Nigerian society is tightly structured. It is the lack of this structure that baffles so many Nigerians about British society. It was why even Akin, who thought of England as his second home, called the country decadent. I pressed him on this. He floundered for a moment and rather lamely suggested liberal homosexual laws and teenagers with green hair. But it isn't what he meant. He meant that in Britain it is possible, as happened recently, for an old woman to freeze to death in her council flat and for her son, just back from a holiday in Tenerife, to blame the government's inadequate pension allowance. This is inconceivable in Nigeria.

And yet what is conceivable in Nigeria is a base level of brutality that would shock most Europeans. My own attitude towards this brutality was ambivalent. Consider the way Akin treated his clerk, who he employed to answer the phone, type letters and carry his books to court. Undoubtedly the clerk wasn't the brightest of men, which was why he was only a clerk. He couldn't type even a simple letter without making the most elementary mistakes time and again. Whenever this happened Akin would shout abuse at him in front of his clients. If Shade was also present she would take off where he had stopped. One wouldn't have thought he was a human being at such times. But at least he was never hit. The housegirl, a recent addition to the household, was less fortunate.

A short, stocky, ugly girl in a loose-fitting cotton dress, she had been brought round late one night by one of Akin's relatives. She claimed to be eighteen but looked younger, and her command of English was shaky to say the least. She had with her a small bundle which contained her only other article of clothing, another loose-fitting cotton dress that was only slightly better than the one she was wearing. Except for the fact that she was paid a meagre N15 a week, most of which she sent to her parents in the east, she may as well have been a slave. She was up every morning at dawn, and since she slept on a mat in the corner of the living room she was invariably the last to go to bed. All the day long and half the night she was kept busy, seven days a week. Not only was she required to look after the baby, she had to cook, clean the house, wash all the clothes and generally be at the beck and call of all and sundry. If she was only shouted at she was lucky. More than once she was slapped in my presence.

It is easy to be repelled by this kind of behaviour by people who, one feels, ought to know better. I was certainly repelled. And yet, after only six weeks in the country, I came perilously close to doing it myself. Why? Because it was what everybody else did; and because it is the easiest thing in the world to treat a human being in this way: there have to be sanctions against such behaviour for human beings not to treat one another in such a fashion. And, finally, because it is a display of power. Nigeria is a society divided in terms of money, not class. Money is everything. The more money you have the greater your power. It is that straightforward. The mere fact of having money makes you important, and the more you have the more important you are. How you acquire that money is your own affair; it is enough that you have it. This means that anything goes. The clerk and the housegirl, like my uncle's houseboy, expected to be shouted at and beaten up because they were powerless, they had no money. If the positions were reversed they themselves would do the same. It never took long for Europeans, despite their ideas of equality and democracy, to fall into the same kind of behaviour.

And yet the absence of class makes possible another kind of democracy. I remember somebody asking me why the British miners, who were on strike at the time, talked so much about defending their jobs for the future of their sons. Didn't they want their sons to do better? Were they content to spend their lives underground only so that their children could follow them? It didn't make sense. I tried to explain that in Britain a miner's son couldn't conceive of going to university, of becoming a lawyer or a doctor: it wouldn't be among his options. The question wouldn't even arise. Universities were for the middle classes. Knowing your class meant knowing your place. In this sense Nigeria is a more open society. The way you speak does not determine the way you will be treated. It is this fluidity that makes it an exciting country. It was Segun who told me of the cook's son who became a millionaire. He was apparently one of the boys we used to pluck mangoes with in the compound of St Saviour's. He had somehow found his way to England where he had done a course in stained-glass. It was a perceptive choice. He returned to Nigeria in the middle of the oil-boom when the *nouveaux riches* were busy constructing their elaborate houses. I saw many of these houses. The most spectacular had a flyover to the living room on the first floor. Stained-glass became a vogue. He made a killing. Now he lives in his own house in Ikoyi and employs a cook.

8

EXTENDING MY VISA had been no problem. Remi had given me an escort to the appropriate office. My escort was the same soldier who had met me at the airport. He said that he had just come back from the hospital, where his wife had given birth to their first child. Unfortunately the baby had died because he hadn't been able to get her to the hospital in time. It happened like this: she had gone into labour in the early hours of the morning. Halfway between his house and the hospital his car had stalled. He spent the next hour trying to flag down a vehicle but without success: even though there was plenty of traffic they must have thought he was an armed robber. I offered my condolences and felt badly that he should then be put out for my sake.

Remi had also given me the balance of the money and the address of a colleague of his in Warri. To get to Warri meant doubling back to Benin and then turning south. At Warri motor-park I was lucky to find a soldier who knew the person I was looking for and he gave the taxi driver instructions. Even so we had the usual difficulties finding the place. I was finally dropped in front of a guest house. There was a man sweeping the porch. I asked him for directions.

The house was easy to spot. There was an armed guard

patrolling the front. The captain offered me a beer and then busied himself on the phone. He seemed to be organizing a party for that evening. When he wasn't on the phone he made little attempt at conversation. One hour passed; two hours; three hours. He offered me another drink. Another hour later he offered me some dried fish. As I ate he kept glancing at his watch. When I had finished he said:

'What are your movements?'

'I think I'll stay in the guest house down the road,' I said.

He looked relieved. 'Good. I have to go out in a while.'

I got up. 'Remi sends his regards,' I said.

'Yes, I'll see him in Lagos next week.'

I went back to the guest house. It was the first time I had been refused hospitality, but I wasn't surprised: it was a reflection of my state of mind.

The man I had spoken to earlier was busy polishing glasses behind the bar. I booked a room, had a shower, and went back to the bar for a drink. I couldn't shake off my continuing depression. I decided to push on to Aba the next day. Akin had given me the address of a friend of his, a lawyer. I would get a better reception there.

I decided to go into town. Warri consists of a single main road packed either side with hotels and drinking parlours to service the foreigners who work at the oil refinery. I was walking past a place called 'Hotel Havana' when a woman called out, 'Hey, *oyinbo*, come.' She was standing at the entrance smoking a cigarette.

'You want to drink beer?' she asked. It seemed as good a place as any.

We sat at the counter. She was dressed in tight-fitting blue jeans and a white blouse and high heels. She had three small incisions under each eye, probably made by a native doctor as a result of a childhood illness. The music came from a small radio behind the counter. A group of young men were crowded round the one-armed bandit. A single unshaded light bulb hung from the ceiling. The place had a desolate air.

'You like me?' she asked.

'You're very pretty. What's your name?'

'Charity.'

'And you have two sisters called Faith and Hope.'

She laughed. 'How do you know?'

'Never mind.'

She drank from the bottle and wiped her lips with the back of her hand.

'I like *oyinbo* and they like me,' she said. 'I don't like Africa man. They are too rough. Always too much heavy sex. All night they disturb you. *Oyinbo* is different.'

'I see.'

'So you take me to your hotel?'

'How much?'

'Fifty naira.' It was my turn to laugh.

'Is too much?'

'Yes.'

'But I will give you good loving. All my customers are satisfied with me. You don't like my body?' She took my hand and placed it on her small breast.

'I have no money,' I said.

'But *oyinbo* has money. Buy me another beer.' I did so.

'My last boyfriend was German and my best friend in Port Harcourt is Indian. I like Indians. Their skin is golden and they have fine hair. But they are different from us. They have a different religion.' She touched the crucifix round her neck.

'And what happened to the German?' I asked.

'He went home. He was engineer and his job finish. Every night he come here to drink beer. Drink, drink, drink.' She made a noise with her mouth and shook her head. 'Thirty naira,' she said.

'No, I'm sorry, I have no money.' I got up. 'I have to go.'

'What of tomorrow?'

'Yes, maybe tomorrow.'

As I prepared for bed there was a knock on the door. It was the barman.

'Everything all right?' he asked.

'Yes, fine.'

He hesitated a moment, then: 'The money here is not good. Only N100 a month. I want to join the army. They will give me more money.'

'N100 is not much,' I agreed.

'The captain is your friend?'

'In a manner of speaking.'

'Please, help me talk to him.'

'Okay,' I said. It was simpler to lie.

'Thank you.' He started to go, then: 'Can I bring you beer?'

'No.'

I got up early and went for breakfast. The barman had become the waiter. When I finished he became the cashier. On my way out he said:

'Please, I hope you haven't forgotten what we discussed last night?'

'No.'

'Thank you. Safe journey.'

To get to Aba I had to change at Port Harcourt. I was now in densely populated oil-palm country. The plantations of palm trees were set out in neat rectangular blocks on either side of the road stretching as far as one could see. The taxi driver, a big man, hunched over the driving wheel and slammed his foot on the accelerator. As we were pulling into Aba we narrowly avoided an accident. An oncoming vehicle, overtaking another, just missed the bonnet. Both drivers hit their brakes at the same time, which brought them face-to-face. The other started apologizing but the taxi driver, cursing furiously, spat in his face. He caught him in the eye. The passengers found this hilarious but the violence of it made me nervous: my stomach tightened and I felt sick. As we moved on the man in the front seat congratulated the driver on his aim and wondered why he hadn't used the leather whip he kept tucked behind the visor.

Olu was a tall, thin man, roughly my height and build. He had a rasping voice and a bad eye. He told me later that he had been in a motor accident and a piece of the windscreen had lodged in his eye. He had spent six months in a hospital in America without result. Now he was blind in that eye.

He lived in an upstairs flat across the road from his office. As it was lunchtime we went there to eat. He shared the flat with a fourteen-year-old boy called Isaac. Isaac was a relation of his who had been sent to stay with him. This is not an unusual arrangement. In return for cooking and cleaning, Olu sent him to school. But the relationship was not wholly a material one, or even primarily so: as a man with a position in the world, a successful man, he was an example for Isaac to emulate.

After we had eaten we went to his bedroom for a smoke. We talked about the east, where he had lived all his life despite his Yoruba background. His family is well-known in Lagos. His uncle, a doctor, often used to call on my father. I tested out my idea of the necessity for true egalitarianism if Nigeria was going to be able to successfully exploit its phenomenal resources. Igbo society, from what I understood, proved my point. Among Nigeria's major tribes they were unique in possessing a truly open and egalitarian society. It was traditionally a society without kings and in which birth counted for very little; in Lugard's frame of reference, they were 'still in the patriarchal stage, lacking any but the most rudimentary communal organization'. That Lugard had misrepresented them need not concern us here. More than one Igbo writer has already pointed out that Igbo society was in fact highly structured but that people were judged by their achievements, not their background. It was this flexibility that made them so receptive to missionary activity. One of the most striking sights on the journey from Warri had been the abundance of Christian, mainly Catholic, churches.

The relatively high rate of Igbo literacy meant that, at the time of Independence, it was they who effectively ran the country: it was they who filled the civil service, the teaching posts and the upper echelons of the armed forces. Their contribution in all spheres of public life was disproportionate to their numbers, today reckoned at fifteen million but probably much more. But this dominance was also their undoing. Within four years of Independence there was a political crisis as the ruling Northern Party was accused of ballot-rigging and large-scale corruption. In January, 1966, the army struck. I remember my father listening to the early morning news on the very day. I knew something was up because although it was gone eight he was still in his dressing gown.

If the intention of the Igbo officers had been to bring some form of stability to a country plundered by five years of irresponsible leadership they were mistaken. What it did do was stir up tribal mistrust. Within seven months there was a counter-coup by northern officers and the massacre of thousands of Igbos living in the north. My father had a book of photographs showing some of the atrocities. The one I remember most vividly was of a woman in her thirties who had been forced to eat one of her eyes at knife-point. Civil war was only a matter of time as Igbos from all over fled home.

Olu had been in and around Aba for the duration of the war, which dragged on for three and a half years. He agreed with me when I suggested that the defeat of Biafra, as the break-away state was called, represented the triumph of reaction over progress. Because of this he didn't think the matter was done with. The combined forces of the rest of Nigeria had won a battle, not a war. 'We taught them a lesson they will never forget,' Bature had said in an unguarded moment when we had discussed the subject; but what is happening in the east today is a resurgence which might very well spell a new round of conflict. Aba itself, a large town, has earned itself the nickname 'Taitwo', after Taiwan. It is said – and Olu confirmed it – that there is nothing one cannot obtain here, from radio sets to spare parts for aeroplanes, all locally produced. I even came across a story in one of the newspapers about an Aba mechanic who had cobbled together a motor car from scratch. Such dynamism is the key to the country's future. It is this alone which will release it from its crippling dependence on foreign imports.

But Olu didn't think there would be another war. He pointed out that the oil, which accounts for 95 per cent of the country's foreign exchange, will run out by the end of the century. When that happens the north will simply let the south go. In the meantime the east is being heavily penalized. The bulk of the oil revenue is being diverted to the north to build up industry and open new schools. There are even new refineries being built in the north, which is crazy when you think about it: crude oil has to be piped thousands of miles into the interior to be refined before coming all the way back again to be shipped overseas. According to Olu the refineries in the north will eventually refine Saudi Arabian crude. It is worth pointing out that in 1977, the date for which I was able to get figures, the largest number of non-Saudi Muslims to make the pilgrimage to Mecca came from Nigeria. In the Muslim world Nigeria is an important country. A few weeks after I left the country the new government secretly joined the Islamic Organization Conference. Southern Nigerians learnt about it for the first time in the foreign press. The present disturbances in the universities – May/June, 1986 – are the result of southern fears of an emerging Islamic state.

I was pleased to have established an immediate rapport with Olu after my shabby reception in Warri. After he returned to the office I went to lie down in the spare room. Isaac wandered in and sat on the bed. He produced a piece of paper. Four words were written on it: Ignorance, Suspect, Issue, Offence. He asked me to define them. I did so using examples that would be familiar to him. Then he asked me to teach him some English words which would help him become a lawyer. He wanted to be a lawyer like Olu, he said, to have an office full of big books and to earn lots of money. He didn't want to be a doctor. That was too easy. All doctors knew was how to stick needles into people. I told him to read as much as he could and develop the habit of using a dictionary. He nodded gravely as I spoke. Then he asked me what I was doing in Aba. I spread my map on the bed and traced my route so far.

'You mean you have been to all these places?' he asked incredulously.

'Would you like to travel in Nigeria?'

'Very much. And I want to learn all the languages so that if anybody calls me a bastard I will know that he is abusing me.'

He asked me how much it was costing me. I gave him a rough estimate.

'Wonderful!' he exclaimed. Then he asked me how much it had cost to fly from London to Lagos. I told him. His jaw dropped.

'Then I must eat book if I want to go overseas,' he said.

It started raining, a sudden downpour which brought with it a cool breeze. Somewhere nearby a church service was in progress. Isaac asked me if it was true that some Europeans had white hair. I said that it was so. Olu came back. His shirt was soaked. He called Isaac and started shouting at him.

In the morning, anxious for me to see the sights, Olu dropped me off at the Museum of Colonial History, an uninspired affair consisting of a number of rooms full of photographs laid out in chronological order. The only substantial object was a worm-eaten desk used by a colonial officer at the turn of the century. The Museum shops weren't much better: half-a-dozen huts with overpriced native crafts. I bought a wooden paper knife and decided to wander round the town.

It was in Aba that I found, not surprisingly, the first decent bookshop of my journey so far. It catered largely for the educational market, packed as it was from floor to ceiling with text books, but it also had a good literature section. This included cheap English-language paperbacks from Nigerian publishing houses. They were unashamedly directed at the mass market. The most dynamic of these publishing houses appeared to be the Enugu-based Fourth Dimension Publishers with a series called 'The African Viewpoint'. The garish covers invariably included pictures of half-naked women. The most intriguing of them, *No Easier Road* by E. Okolo, was dominated by a photograph of a blonde-haired, blue-eyed, big-busted white woman. I read the blurb on the back:

She fought him violently, scratching, kicking and biting . . . Her sorrowful yelp of pain was cut off as he slammed the

139

hockey-stick, this time against her skull and felt brain and blood splash all over his body. This gruelling fight, dastardly masochistic wrenching of life is the matrix of 'No Easier Road'.

Sex orgies, violent robberies and blood-chilling murders climax this suspense-filled adventure. The actions keep you going till the last word.

I bought it.

I read the novel in one sitting and thoroughly enjoyed it. The plot was simple: a gang of criminals rob a bank, fall out over the division of the spoils, and start killing each other as the police close in. Crudely written and often gratuitously violent, it was brought to the boil every now and then with detailed descriptions of sex solely designed to titillate. One of the most revolting scenes, and the least convincing, is an account of a castration in which the victim, waking from a drug-induced sleep, 'watched her throw the balls into her mouth like they were tablets. Then with a sinking feeling – a feeling that gave way to an exploding rage he watched her chew the balls in relish and wash the particles down with whisky.'

The dominating influence is clearly the Mickey Spillane/James Hadley Chase school of hardboiled American writing. The novel is full of phrases like, 'A wrong step and I'll drill you full of holes'; 'If you don't want me to blast out your guts better get away now'; 'There are times when I think the whole lousy cops we have in this city are mugs.'

Sex is his real speciality. And yet his treatment of it, which is never coy, is too vital to be called pornographic. The woman is described in vivid detail:

Her body was the colour of flowing brass, a colour that never failed to captivate him. She had large, firm breasts that stood out like beckoning ripe pawpaw. The nipples stood erect and defiant with roseates that alternated between a captivating brass and a tantalising faint-red . . .

Which isn't to say that her role is merely passive:

> She grabbed his startling piston of manhood . . . She toyed with it – weighing it in her palm, using her expert fingers to discover the promise it held for her. The effect was stimulating. Her eyes grew wide as saucers – with a mixture of awe and startled curiosity as that piece of manhood grew to fearful proportions. It was now a turgid, thumping cock that was stubborn with passion and which showed no sign of budging until it had satisfied its immediate desire.

It is difficult not to be seduced by the vigour of the prose and the sometimes startling originality of phase. Lacking pretension, it is in contrast to the often ponderous novels of his more celebrated compatriots with a background in English literature. The writer is not burdened with a message; he couldn't give a damn about the colonial experience or the problems of the bourgeoisie caught between tradition and modernity. His novel has an honesty and freshness lacking in the novels of the Western-educated, angst-ridden writers more familiar to the European reader. The irony is that Bature's friend in Kano, the one who read only American pulp fiction, wouldn't have even glanced at Okolo's novel.

Even Okolo's Americanisms, strange as they may appear at first sight, are part of the Nigerian reality. The cities are full of young men and women in tight jeans and dark glasses who have grown up on a diet of Hollywood movies and who imagine that America is populated with gun-toting criminals who speak in clipped sentences when they aren't blasting each other to oblivion. Such people are as Nigerian as anyone else. But they do violence to the myth of the unspoilt

African in the village, otherwise known as the noble savage, who alone is regarded as authentic. A large part of his authenticity lies in the fact that he is 'traditional'; i.e., he represents the age-old values of Africa which existed before the coming of the white man. This is nonsense. Such an Africa never existed. It is a myth. There is no such thing as 'traditional' in this sense of the word except in the minds of those who have a need for it. All societies, in order to survive, are constantly changing and adapting. 'Traditional' societies, synonymous with static societies, are those which buckle under the first onslaught from outside. History is littered with examples of such societies. The story of their descendants, isolated, impoverished, more often than not hunted to extinction, is not a pleasant one. The majority of the older generation of the Nigerian intelligentsia, who certainly ought to know better, refuse to see this. Obsessed with the notion that they have somehow betrayed their heritage, their 'roots', by studying in the institutions of the former colonial power, they spend an inordinate amount of time and energy flagellating themselves in public as unworthy Africans. If they really believed what they claimed they would divest themselves of their motor cars and their university jobs, throw away their typewriters, and settle down in the most backward village they could find. They could then spend the rest of their lives grubbing in the soil for a pittance and beating their wives whenever they were bored, which would be often. But like most people they want both, so they attend conferences in London and Paris and New York and sentimentalize the life of the peasant, whose already loaded back is made to carry yet another burden.

The other novels were less vigorous, but no less amusing. An interesting feature of all of them was their predominantly urban setting. Not for them the village scene of ponderous old men issuing words of ancient wisdom handed down through the generations, which has itself become a tradition in the more upmarket novels. It is the cities, after all, with their appalling contradictions and their terrifying levels of violence, which are the future.

In the evening Olu told me that he had met an old schoolfriend of mine who, hearing that I was around, had arranged to come and see me the following day. His name was David. I had been talking about him with Akin just before I had left Lagos. I remembered him as one of the best tennis players in the school and a notorious womanizer.

Olu brought him round in the middle of the afternoon. He hadn't changed at all. He still looked the playboy: the expensive clothes and the dark glasses. He had a woman in tow. He introduced her as Angie. She clearly wasn't his wife. Olu gave Isaac money to buy some beer and then left us to talk.

David hadn't seen or even been in contact with his family throughout the war. He told me how much trouble he had had readjusting after he had returned. Then he had gone to London to study Law. Now he had his own practice. He had done his Youth Service in Kano shortly after the Maitatsine riots. He had been on one of the tribunals. It was part of his duty to visit the mass graves of the rioters. When he stepped on them he had had the sensation of stepping on human bellies.

Later we went out. We called in at an hotel owned by his family. It was here that Angie was staying. Then we went to his house. He explained that Angie, who was nineteen, had simply turned up at his office one day. She had lived in England all her life and had only recently come to Nigeria because her parents had sent for her. She said she was an actress.

David's wife, a doctor, was still at the clinic. I met her later. She was a petite woman in her twenties. The housegirl prepared a meal. I glanced at the titles on the bookshelf. It was filled with American blockbusters. There wasn't an African novel in sight. Afterwards we went into the garden for a smoke. He pointed to the next house, also owned by his father. It had been turned into a nursery. His mother, who ran it, employed an Indian woman in order to attract both the expatriate community and the resident Nigerian bourgeoisie. In another of the novels I had picked up, *Climate of Corruption* by Labo Yari, I had read the following:

> Let me tell you one thing, there are people living here who take their children daily to Ikoyi to kindergartens and schools. Not because there are no schools or kindergartens in this part of Lagos, no, simply because Ikoyi is synonymous with colonialism. '

In other words, twenty-five years of Independence has not been long enough to inculcate a sense of national identity sufficiently strong to displace the habit of dependency. Or has it?

It happened that while I was in Nigeria the national under-17 football team, the Golden Eaglets, had won the junior World Cup, held in China, by beating Germany by two goals to one. The country went wild. On their return each player was presented with a colour television set and the guarantee of free education up to university level. It was even suggested that their day of victory be celebrated annually as a public holiday. My first inclination was to dismiss it all as rather excessive, but that would have been to have missed an important connection.

The television stations showed endless repeats of the goal that clinched the match. One of the Nigerian forwards, finding himself in possession of the ball in front of the German goalmouth but not properly balanced, could have kicked out wildly and hoped for the best. He did something else. He held on to the ball long enough to regain his balance, confronted and evaded two defenders, and then slammed the ball home from a difficult angle. At that moment I caught a glimpse of the future. It was encapsulated in that young man on a football field in far-away China and it was pure confidence.

His youth was everything. To be his age in Nigeria means to have been born into an already independent State, to be born without the handicap of those who grew up in a dependent territory. He is not troubled by the sneaking suspicion of his own possible inferiority, which is the damaging legacy of the colonial experience. It is the reason why the subsequent leaders behaved as irresponsibly as they did the moment they assumed power. Let me be quite clear about this: twenty-five years ago, even ten years ago, it would have been impossible for a Nigerian football team to have won that match, although it would have been conceivable for an individual athlete to have broken any number of world records. We are not here talking about the exception, the freak. A football match is not won by the lone individual. Behind that young man there were ten others, all of them equally confident.

Am I not guilty of reading too much into an insignificant event? Doesn't it go against all the facts, the 'facts' being the daily accumulation of evidence that Nigeria simply doesn't work, that Nigerians can't even run a hotel properly let alone a country? True, there are constant power failures, a continuous shortage of running water, an inefficient postal service and an unreliable telephone system; policemen are rude, officials rarely know their jobs and the roads are in an appalling state of disrepair. Despite its huge reservoirs of high-quality petroleum the country is in debt, the hospitals are out of essential drugs and there is a shortage of everything from food to motor cars. But to say this is to say nothing new. It is part of the definition of the so-called 'Third World'. This is precisely what makes it so dangerous. While it is true that one sees all these things it is also true that one is conditioned to see them. What one doesn't see are the more nebulous but equally important signs that profound changes are taking place. It is at precisely this point that writers like Festus Iyayi and Ben Okri must be seen as a wider movement, belonging as they do to that same generation as the young footballers.

Meanwhile, David's wife came home and we returned to the hotel. Angie, who had nowhere to go and nobody to see, was waiting where we had left her. David and I made fitful conversation but having brought each other up to date there was little left to say. Sixteen years is a long time.

It was nearly midnight when he dropped me back at Olu's place. I had to rouse Isaac from his makeshift bed on the living-room floor. I decided to leave for Calabar the following day. I still had a long way to go. I wanted to reach Maiduguri in the far north-east before turning south again. In the morning Olu cooked my breakfast, another instance of the kind of hospitality that I found so touching: two fried eggs, a flask of coffee, bread and butter. The eggs, which he covered with a plate, had congealed by the time I had washed and dressed. On my way out I saw Isaac wolfing them down over the kitchen sink after he had cleared up. Eggs are expensive in Nigeria.

At the motor-park, as we waited for the taxi to fill up, there was a startling sight: a procession of a dozen men and women, chained together, walking single-file behind a man with a bell. Bringing up the rear, with a chipped wooden bowl in his hands, another, younger man solicited for alms. They were all dressed in rags and had the vacant stare of the insane. One of my fellow-passengers explained that the man with the bell was a native healer.

The journey to Calabar took three hours. No sooner had I stepped out of the taxi than I was surrounded by small Japanese motorcycles raising dust and creating a fearful noise. This turned out to be the most popular form of public transport. The roads were full of these motorcycles weaving in and out of the traffic. Often they carried more than they were designed for, the engines protesting under the accumulated weight. It was not unusual to see a woman riding side-saddle with a baby on her back, shopping on her lap and a toddler squeezed into the space between her and the driver. It seemed a dangerous if cheap way to travel.

I had been given the names of two people at the university, both of them in the Department of Theatre Arts. I found one of them. He was on his way home. He apologized that he didn't have his car with him. which had been in an accident a few months ago and was presently at the garage undergoing extensive repairs.

He lived nearby in a university-owned apartment with his wife and two children. All the furniture was stamped 'Unical' (University of Calabar): cheap, mass-produced wooden chairs and tables. The only expensive item was a huge colour television set which dominated the sitting room. He was also something of a painter: all four walls were crammed with his oil paintings which, if not terribly well executed, at least provided plenty of colour. I was given the spare bedroom. It was opposite the bathroom and doubled as his study. We had lunch and went out. He wanted to show me the town.

We stopped at a small store. He introduced me to the owner, who was his brother. They didn't look much alike – Uche was small and dark; his brother was tall and light – but 'brother' in Nigeria is an elastic term: they may have simply been from the same village or clan, but as Igbos in foreign territory they are automatically brothers. Bottles of beer and tumblers were produced, the radio was turned low, and I was effectively forgotten as they huddled together and engaged in a lengthy conversation.

Afterwards we strolled down to the beach. It was from these shores, at the height of the Atlantic slave trade in the eighteenth century, that many Africans journeyed under appalling conditions to the New World. As evening fell and the canoes drifted peacefully towards the shore to unload the last of their catch it seemed that one ought to have been able to hear the cries of the captives rise up from the ground. There are times when one feels, or hopes, that the earth itself demands retribution for the suffering of human beings.

We talked about literature. Uche was a poet and playwright who wrote in Igbo because, he said, he was more interested in reaching a local audience than satisfying a European one. I was pleased to hear him say this. But there were problems. He wanted to return to his village in order to communicate directly with the people but it would be impossible to support his family there. Besides, if he were to return nobody would listen to him. Having escaped it once – all the way to London, in fact, where he had spent four years writing a doctoral thesis – they would assume that his return was a mark of his failure.

The market traders started packing up for the day. We turned from the water's edge and walked back to the main road. By the time we got back into town it was dark. Uche suggested we try a nightclub. He said that if I wanted a woman – I hadn't said anything to indicate that I did – it would be easy because Calabar women were 'cheap', a fact which everybody knew. Even married women would jump into bed with you for a small consideration. There was a woman ahead of us. She was walking slowly and swaying her hips. As we drew level with her Uche said, in his high, squeaky voice: 'Hey, fine woman, won't you come with us?' She didn't answer. 'It's because we haven't got a car, isn't it?' he sneered; then, to me: 'Don't mind her. She's stupid. If we had a car she would be more than happy to follow us.' I thought he was being crass but didn't say so. We arrived at the club. They wanted N10 at the gate. Uche argued with them but they wouldn't budge. He said he knew of a cheaper place. We stopped a couple of motorcycle taxis. It started drizzling. We were dropped outside the club. The building was in darkness. A few women stood outside the front gate. One of them explained that there was a strike. We went into a drinking parlour nearby and had a beer. I was bored and tired. My canvas shoes were soaked and I was terrified of catching a cold. I suggested we call it a day. Uche only very reluctantly agreed. I got even wetter on the way home. It was almost midnight by the time we let ourselves in. His wife, asleep on the living-room couch, got up and served us a meal.

I lay awake a long time that night. I couldn't sleep because I wanted a shit; I couldn't shit because the toilet was bunged up. There was no running water in the flat and nobody had bothered to fill up the cistern and flush it. The stench from the accumulated waste, dried hard in places and covered with used toilet paper, filtered under my door.

All the next day long we hung around the flat. Uche said he reserved Sundays for his family. Now and then he disappeared into his bedroom to worship at his shrine. I was intrigued but it wasn't until much later in the day that I finally managed to persuade him to let me see it. He thought I would make fun of him. There wasn't much to it: a few badly executed masks, an assortment of fly whisks, a wooden bowl containing pieces of chalk. He said that although he had been brought up a Catholic he had since renounced Catholicism for the religion of his ancestors. I didn't laugh; I didn't think it was funny. I thought it was probably wrong-headed but harmless. My attitude had

149

nothing to do with the supposed power of the gods – all gods are powerful – but with the attempt on his part to resuscitate a way of life, and the gods which had supported that life, that has since been overtaken by history. He reminded me of those people in Britain who gather every year at Stonehenge: history may have rendered the gods ineffectual, but perhaps it is just as well that there are always a few who keep alive that memory which is history.

In the evening a colleague of his dropped in briefly. He was also a writer. I knew of him by reputation as an experimental novelist. When I hear the word experimental applied to a writer I run a mile. He had a copy of his latest novel with him. I persuaded him to give it to me on the understanding that I would review it for a British paper, but I only had to read the first four sentences of the opening paragraph to realize that I would do nothing of the sort:

> Any great event is necessarily complex. Any happening, that is, which is distinguished. Is great, because it is powered by an immense vitality. Perpetual livingness there is in it.

Give me the straightforward, unpretentious honesty of *No Easier Road* any day.

We talked some politics. He was also a Marxist. I had come to understand that to call oneself a Marxist in Nigeria has more to do with a commitment to nationalism than to a specific political ideology. He said that Nigeria ought to cut itself off from the rest of the world, as China and Cuba had done, in order to force the pace of industrialization. The Igbos, a naturally self-reliant people, would lead the way. Hadn't I noticed how few beggars there were in the Igbo country compared with the north? An Igbo man won't beg. He'll ask you if you have a job of work for him to do and

150

he'll carefully save up until he has enough to branch out into small business of his own. The Hausa man, on the other hand, will put his poverty down to the will of Allah and continue to live in misery. That is why the north is reactionary; that is why there will never be a genuine revolution in the country.

9

JUST OUTSIDE CALABAR, on my way north again, we were stopped at a road-block. This was nothing new. Between the army and the police and the civilian tax-collectors one was liable to be stopped at fairly regular intervals. A group of young men in filthy clothes and not a pair of shoes between them had erected a makeshift barrier across the road: a plank of wood with upturned nails.

'Tax,' one of them said. A passenger produced a dog-eared passport-size photograph. The men scrutinized it and waved us on.

I changed taxis at a place called Katsina Ala, a town on one of the tributaries of the Benue River. By now it was late afternoon. Once more the tropical rainforest had given way to open plains, and the frantic, cluttered, corrugated-iron villages to the isolated clusters of thatched huts. It wasn't difficult to see why the colonial authorities had much preferred the north to the south. Not only is it more peaceful: in certain respects the people are more civilized. This is a dangerous word to use, but it will have to do. The reason is to be found in their greater sense of continuity with the past, for which Islam itself is responsible. Northerners come across as much more self-reliant than their southern counterparts: while it is true that one of the lasting results of so much missionary activity among the southerners has given them a head-start in terms of twentieth-century life, it is also the case that it has left them with a species of schizophrenia which goes a long way to account for the levels of brutality that is a dominant feature of life in the south. The average northerner has not suffered the disruption of the southerner. In terms of religion alone they can look back to an unbroken history of a thousand years or more. And it is precisely their heritage, with its learning and its cultural achievements, that made it possible for the north to successfully resist the intrusion of the Christian missionaries. It is not necessary for the average northerner to be conscious of this heritage. It is enough that they belong to it, that it is part of the climate in which they grow up. One can see it in their behaviour. It is significant, for instance, that I never once heard the word *oyinbo* applied to me in all the time I was in the north. This was because, at a profound level, I did not pose a challenge to their safety or their security. I was peripheral; I was unimportant; I didn't matter.

It was dark when we pulled into Wukari. The motor-park was ablaze with the headlamps of arriving and departing vehicles as they weaved in and out of the milling crowd of travellers and hawkers. It wasn't at first clear whether there would be a connection to Yola that night. I was directed to one taxi, then another, then a third. It was the last which proved to be the one I wanted. I stood by the front passenger door and smoked a cigarette. The young man already inside came out to join me. He carried his sandals in his hand and explained that one of them had just broken. He caught me looking at a hawker selling bits of coconut from a tray balanced on his head. He called the boy over and told me to select what I wanted. Presently the driver turned up and we set off.

There was little traffic on the road. I soon realized why. In all the miles I had so far travelled I had become used to great stretches of road where the surface had simply crumbled away. Many of these roads had been built only in the last ten years, but the contractors had skimped on materials in order to increase their profit margins so that after the first rains the fragile coating of tar had been washed away. The corruption associated with road-building in Nigeria is legendary. In a book I was reading at the time, *A Nation In Custody* by Naiwu Osahon, I had come across the following:

A Lagos state ministry has just discovered that Anthony village has been tarred at a cost of several millions. On paper yes, because the millions had disappeared into some functionaries private scheme while Anthony village continues to degenerate into abject neglect, untarred like Ajegunle, Mushin, Maroko, Makoko . . .

This particular stretch was the worst yet. It didn't help that we were being driven by a maniac. He was a small, wiry, talkative man who seemed to find it impossible to keep his eyes on the road as he carried on a running conversation with the man behind. Each time we hit a pothole there was a tremendous crashing sound as the undercarriage scraped the ground, but no matter how many times this happened he couldn't be induced to slow down. In the meantime I was engaged in conversation with the man with the broken sandal. He told me he was from Cameroon and was on his way to visit his brother in Yola.

It was midnight when we arrived in Yola. It turned out that the Cameroonian's brother didn't actually live in the town but a few miles outside. The driver refused to take us there. The Cameroonian directed him to a nightclub.

It was an open-air club with a concrete dancing area in one corner. A few men imagined they were body-popping to a Michael Jackson record. The only women about were prostitutes. Every now and then a couple would disappear into one of the cubicles that ringed the open space but otherwise there seemed to be little connection between the sexes. The men danced for the benefit of each other; there was no suggestion of sexuality. This gave the whole scene a nihilistic quality, made more unreal by the flashing strobe lights, half of which didn't work.

The Cameroonian directed me to an empty table and called the waiter for beer. We were soon joined by one of the women. She didn't seem to be soliciting for custom so much as taking the opportunity to be bought a drink. I obliged. She drank straight from the bottle, thanked us and left.

The Cameroonian leaned forward to talk to me above the din of the music, which was deafening. He said he was excited by the fact that I was a writer. There were many things he could show me which would help me with my book. He would be useful because he had a way with white men. He liked them and they liked him. Once, a few years ago, he had befriended an American who was also interested in learning about Africa. He had taken him across the border into Cameroon and shown him a magical lake. The lake was used by the people of his tribe to judge cases of adultery, theft and murder. It never failed. Many people had died in that lake. No matter how hard the authorities searched they could never find the bodies. He could show me many other things besides. He had shown the American many things. The American had been his very good friend. They had become like brothers. He even wanted to take him back to America with him when it was time for him to leave. He, the Cameroonian, had gone with him to the airport. They had both stood on the tarmac in each other's arms. The American had been the last to board the plane. Just before they closed the doors for take-off he had rushed out to say goodbye again. Because of him the flight had been delayed. Only the other day he had received a letter from him. He had the letter in his pocket. He took it out and showed it to me. It was with a bundle of other letters. He went everywhere with them. They were his most valuable possessions. He took the letter out of the envelope, spread it on the round, metal table, and passed it to me. It was too dark to read. I gave it back to him. He put it in the envelope. Yes, he could help me with my book. I should leave everything to him. He could arrange for me to meet lots of people and see many things. He sat back, smiling. The Michael Jackson record came on again. It seemed to be a favourite. It was gone two o'clock. I was very tired. The Cameroonian called for more beer.

A policeman wandered over to our table and glared at me. He was a big, evil-looking man and so drunk he couldn't hold himself straight. I ignored him. The Cameroonian said: 'Why don't you sit down?' He did so. His huge frame filled the seat and drove the legs further into the sand. He continued to glare at me.

'If you have something you want to say why not say it instead of looking at my friend like that? Don't you see he is a stranger here? He is not used to our ways,' the Cameroonian said. It hadn't occurred to me that there was anything particularly strange about the policeman's 'ways'. The policeman shrugged and stood up. He swayed on his feet and shuffled away. The Cameroonian shook his head.

'I'm tired,' I said.

'Would you like to sleep? Wait here.'

He went over to a nearby table and started talking to one of the women. Every so often they glanced at me. Finally he came back.

'I told her that we are both working for the Lower Benue Basin Authority and that we arrived in Yola too late to meet our boss. I told her that you were very tired and wanted to sleep. She said you can rent her room for N5.' He beckoned the woman over and introduced her as Juliana. She was a tall woman in a cheap cotton dress that fell below her knees.

'You see how we are with these people,' he said, meaning me. 'He bought beer for another woman. You know that these white men don't discriminate among us as we do. But she just went away without asking if she could help him. And then you saw the policeman just now. What will he think of us?'

Juliana looked appropriately downcast. She kept her face averted and told us to follow her. We entered one of the cubicles. There was a bed, a chair, a table. A single unshaded red bulb dangled from the ceiling. A few clothes hung from a nail on the back of the door. I lay on the bed. The Cameroonian asked me if I had money for beer. Juliana continued to look downcast.

'I am so ashamed,' she finally said.

'Why?'

'Because of the way we have treated you. You must think badly of us.'

The Cameroonian had evidently laid it on a bit thick. I asked her about herself. She said she was from Katsina-Ala; that her husband had been killed two years ago in an accident at the factory; and that she had come to Yola to earn money. Her two children lived in Katsina-Ala. They were looked after by her mother-in-law. As she talked I began to drop off.

I woke with first light. Juliana was standing over the bed. She handed me a plastic lunch box containing a piece of soap and sponge.

When I had washed and dressed the Cameroonian came and asked me for N5. I gave it to him. After he had gone Juliana said:

'Your friend is not from Cameroon.'

'How do you know?'

'He is from my place. He can speak Tiv very well. Be careful, he will cheat you.'

I gave her N10. She asked me if she could have my St

Christopher. I explained that it had magical properties for my protection and so I couldn't be separated from it. She understood and didn't press me. The Cameroonian, sandals in hand, came back again and we left.

He had got it into his head that we were going to visit his brother together but I was anxious to be rid of him. I knew he was broke; I didn't believe in his brother; I wanted to push on to Maiduguri. I pretended to suddenly remember an appointment I had in Maiduguri. I promised that I would be back in a couple of days and would meet him at the nightclub. He wasn't stupid; he didn't believe me. I didn't care. He walked me to the motor-park and then went on his way.

The journey to Maiduguri took four hours. It was the most beautiful stretch of country I had travelled so far. I was surprised. Since we were heading in the general direction of the Sahara I had expected semi-desert. But I saw fields of green on one side and mountains on the other. The roadside villages were clean and well-kept.

I had an address at the university of an acquaintance from London. I was dropped at the main gate. With some difficulty I found his department only to be told that he had travelled the previous day and wouldn't be back for a week. I was relieved. I had only come this far to be able to say that I had reached Maiduguri.

The motor-park wasn't far from the university. By mid-afternoon I was in another taxi preparing to return to Yola. On the way out of the motor-park we were flagged down by an elderly man. He came up to me and began shouting in Hausa. While I was trying to figure out what I could have possibly done to him one of my fellow-passengers explained that he wanted to see my tax form. I was getting sick of this charade. I decided to ignore him. This only made him angrier. He was practically screaming at me as he indicated for me to get out. I told the interpreter to inform him that I wasn't a Nigerian citizen but that if he still insisted on seeing my tax form he was welcome to follow me to England; in the meantime he could go to hell. The interpreter laughed. 'So you want to play with these people,' he said. I shrugged. He said something to the old man. This appeared to mollify him. He wagged his finger at me and let me go.

At four o'clock we stopped at a village and we all bundled out. It was time for the Muslims to say their prayers. The first man to finish came over to me, took my hand in his and said something in Hausa. 'I don't understand,' I said. He said something else and laughed and held on to my hand, almost caressing it. I reminded myself that in Nigeria this wasn't unusual.

We stopped again at seven o'clock. We were just outside Yola. Some of the passengers left. The remainder, except the Alhaji and I, dropped off at various points in the town. At the motor-park, as I was collecting my bag from the boot, the Alhaji grabbed hold of me. He said something and laughed. Then he started making a motion of putting food in his mouth. I was on the point of accepting – it was still early and I was hungry – when he suddenly brushed the back of my hand against his stiffened prick. I pulled free. It was difficult to find my way in the darkness. I went out of the main gate, turned, and fell straight into an open gutter. It was one of the few cement gutters I had come across in the country. It was about four feet deep and perfectly dry. I grazed my arm slightly. I scrambled out and walked quickly to the main road. When I looked back I saw no sign of him.

I had something to eat outside the nightclub where women fried yam, plantain and *akara* (bean cakes). As I was smoking a cigarette, Juliana came out.

'Have you seen your friend?' she asked.

'No.'

'He came in the afternoon. He asked me for one naira to repair his shoe.'

'Did you give it to him?'

'Yes.'

She took my bag and we went into the club. Michael Jackson was still blasting out from the huge amplifiers either side of the dance floor. Being a creature of habit I sat at the same table as last night. Juliana took my bag to her room and then came to join me. She drank a bottle of beer and went away. I waited thirty minutes and then went to find her. She was in her room. She was putting on make-up and chatting with a friend. A man was lying on the bed. He looked at me and then at Juliana. Presently he and the girlfriend left. Juliana said:

'That man is my boyfriend.'

'I see.'

She asked me for a cigarette.

'You haven't seen your friend?'

'No.'

'You know I have to go out and earn money. Last night I was sorry for you, that's all.'

It was what I deserved. Why else had I come back if not for a cheap place to sleep before continuing on my journey? There was nothing for it but to go and find a hotel.

On the main road again I stopped a young man and asked him if he knew of somewhere inexpensive. I tried to impress on him that I didn't have a lot of money. He told me to follow him. We walked about a kilometre. At one point we left the main road. In the darkness it was not always possible to avoid the potholes, which were full of water from the rain earlier in the day. We finally reached a hotel. The rooms started from N25. I had little choice. The young man followed me to the room and settled himself in an easy chair. I was exhausted and wanted to write up my notes before going to sleep but I could hardly tell him to go. At the very least I should have offered him a soft drink.

I asked him about himself. He said he was from Enugu, in the east, but that he had come to Yola to work as an apprentice mechanic with his senior brother. He disliked the town. They were backward here, especially in fashion. They were always two or three years behind Enugu. Besides, there was nothing to do. Hadn't I noticed that there was only one two-storey building here? It had been built about five years ago but has remained unoccupied. The neighbours either side and across the road had taken out an injunction against the owner to prevent him occupying it because, they said, he would be able to stand on his balcony and see into their harems. This was the kind of mentality that prevailed here. It was so backward. He couldn't understand it. He asked me for pen and paper.

'This is my address,' he said. He waited for me to reciprocate. Finally I said:

'Do you think you will ever come to England?'

'By God's grace.'

I wrote down my address. He looked at it, repeated it to make sure he had got it right, and then slipped it into his pocket.

'Would you like me to send you something?' I asked.

'Yes.'

'What would you like?'

'I don't mind.'

'But there must be something in particular you would like me to send you.'

'I don't mind,' he repeated. Whatever he had in mind he wasn't saying. It would have been indelicate for him to have said, just as it was indelicate of me to press him. I said nothing further. He stood up.

'Okay, let me be going,' he said. I walked him to the lane and we shook hands.

Alone at last, I scribbled a few notes. It was easy to get out of the habit of keeping my notes up-to-date. All things considered I hadn't done too badly. Then I lay on the bed. When I woke up it was morning. A child was screaming. I went to the window and looked out. Through the hedge that separated the hotel from the next compound a woman was beating a naked child with a switch. She was holding his arm to keep him from running away. She didn't look particularly angry; in fact she was smiling. Two older children looked on impassively.

Halfway to Wukari we switched taxis. This was common practice. It meant the drivers could return to their point of departure and fill up again. A leper was among the passengers in the other taxi. He wore brightly coloured woollen socks and home-made rubber sandals. He walked with great difficulty. Presumably he had no toes. He didn't have any fingers. Between two stumps he clutched a blue plastic bottle of drinking water. For once I was glad I wasn't sitting in the front seat. A young woman had that privilege. I stared for a while at the back of her head before I realized what was wrong: she had been using skin-lightening cream which had left great blotches of yellow where it had peeled into her skin.

We reached Wukari in the early afternoon. Seen by day, it revealed itself as one of the bigger motor-parks. There were hawkers everywhere, many of them women. Most of them carried a baby on their back. They walked endlessly up and down in the tremendous heat trying to interest the travellers in their wares. Now and then they would lift up their blouses and cram a heavy breast into an expectant mouth.

I was directed to the Enugu taxi. I was the only passenger. As the afternoon dragged on and I consumed soft drinks, peanuts, coconut, oranges, guava, it seemed that no one else was going my way. Now and then the driver would wander over to see that I was still there and to complain about the lack of business. I asked him what he thought about the latest coup. He shrugged and pointed to a four-storey building. He said that it had been built in the time of the civilians for the sole purpose of hoarding rice. During the first coup the soldiers had broken into it and given the rice away. That had made them very popular. But things hadn't really improved. A new car tyre now cost N150. His own taxi was off the road. He couldn't afford to repair it. He had hired this one from a friend and right now he was losing money. He shrugged again. He didn't really expect anything to change.

By six o'clock he gave up hoping for a miracle. He would sleep in the taxi overnight. He pointed to a nearby hotel and recommended that I stay there. He would be leaving at four in the morning.

Hotel was too grandiose a word for such a dingy joint. The main room, which had no windows, was lit by a single red bulb, no doubt to hide the dirt. As I waited for the proprietor to return with the appropriate forms, I caught sight of a rat scampering under one of the chairs.

I could choose between two rooms. The first, which was N10, had a bed and a fan; the second, which was N12, had a bed but no fan. But the N12 room had a bathroom, complete with bath-tub and toilet. There was only one drawback: despite the elaborate plumbing there was no running water.

'No fan?' I asked. He shook his head.

'But the N10 room has a fan.'

'Yes.'

It didn't seem to occur to him that he might make a little extra money by putting the fan in the N12 room. What did it matter to me? I took the cheaper room.

After I had written up my notes I went out. Nearby, along the side of the hotel, a woman was frying yam. She was amused by my presence. I bought three pieces and went to sit on the porch, next to an albino: for some reason there were lots of albinos in Wukari. Her son brought me a cup of water. Out of the corner of my eye I saw a rat scurrying along the side of the wall. I finished eating and went back to my room.

I woke at three and went for a wash. The proprietor had left a bucket outside my door as I had asked him to do. I filled it up from an oil-drum outside the washroom. The washroom stank of shit. In the darkness I couldn't see anything. I stood at the entrance and held my breath.

At the motor-park the drivers were beginning to stir. They were standing around in small groups cleaning their teeth with chewing sticks and pissing in corners. I found my driver and bagged the front seat. Gradually it started to fill up. We were on the road within the hour.

Just outside Wukari we stopped for prayers. I fell into conversation with a university graduate who was on his way to Lagos to attend an interview for a Commonwealth University scholarship. He wanted to go to Canada to do a Ph.D. He was anxious to leave the country, at least for a few years. The country was too frustrating. Corruption was killing all initiative. At Ahmadu Bello University in Zaria, where he had studied Economics, the Department of Agriculture had developed a cheap method of making fertilizer from human waste. They applied for a development grant but it was refused: certain influential people were more concerned with their 10 per cent commission from imported fertilizer. In the end the research was abandoned and the people involved took to drink. This was typical. Then there were those well-placed to help the country but who chose instead to throw their money away on wasteful gestures designed to impress the very people they should be helping. He had recently gone back to his village to see his widowed mother. His visit had coincided with the tenth anniversary of the death of a villager whose sons had made good by stealing government money. They threw a Remembrance Party, for which purpose they hired no less than twenty bands. A quarter of a million was spent and yet the village didn't have one decent road.

But, he went on, the villagers were also to blame. They themselves worshipped money. That is why they sucked-up to people. They were impressed by the show of wealth. They wanted to be rich too. They thought that such people should be emulated. Another person I had met, a writer, had put it this way. A mother is walking her child to school on Monday morning. She has spent the weekend washing and ironing his white school uniform so he will look smart for the teacher. But as they are walking along the side of the road a man in a Mercedes splashes them with mud. The mother, instead of berating the driver and cursing the system that allows such disparities of wealth, consoles her child by telling him that one day he, too, will drive such a car.

It doesn't take one long to realize that outward appearances count for a lot in Nigeria, hence Akin's office; and if it is true that Akin needed to display wealth in order to impress potential clients, it is also true that he derived great pleasure from his plush surroundings. It is a trait that many Nigerians themselves deplore:

> The typical Nigerian puts his first air-conditioner in his sitting room until he can afford another one. Then he transfers the second-hand one into his bedroom. It is not our comfort that excites us, it is what others think of us. So we live in one room and park our large expensive car outside it. We are all phoneys, hypocrites ... *(A Nation In Custody)*.

The Muslims finished their prayers and we continued on our way. We arrived in Enugu at noon. The Economics student went off to look for a friend. He invited me along but I declined. I wasn't feeling too well.

I had to wait three hours for the taxi to fill up. A boy selling soft drinks came and stood beside me. I bought a can of Coke I didn't want. I was sick of the stuff. I asked him how much he made in a day. He said he worked from seven in the morning until five in the evening, and if he sold all twenty-four cans he would make N4.50. I spent more than that on cigarettes every day.

The journey to Onitsha took an hour. Onitsha is famous for its market. Before it was burned down in the civil war it was the biggest market in West Africa. It was here, in the late 1940s, that indigenous publishing began in earnest. The now famous Onitsha chapbooks, produced and sold by anyone who managed to pick up a second-hand printing press, were aimed exclusively at the popular market. Their titles give a good indication of their appeal: 'Why Harlots Hate Married Men and Love Bachelors'; 'Sundry Advice About Love'; 'Tales of Rising Corruption'; 'Escape, Arrest and Martyrdom of Lumumba'. They were written, for the most part, by school teachers and government clerks anxious to make a little extra on the side, and they were bought by everybody. Cyprian Ekwensi, later to become one of the most popular of the early generation of Nigerian writers, served his apprenticeship in this way with a pamphlet titled, 'When Love Whispers'. My own favourite is 'Mabel the Sweet Honey that Poured Away' by Speedy Eric: 'Her skin would make your blood flow in the wrong direction. She was so sweet and sexy, knew how to romance. She married at sixteen. But she wanted more fun. Yet it ended at seventeen. And what an end!' No need to say more.

There was a taxi waiting to go to Lagos. It was almost full. Among the passengers was an elderly man who reminded me very much of my grandfather. He was smartly dressed in a pin-stripe suit, a battered derby and leather brogues. A gold chain dangled from his waistcoat and he carried a gold-topped walking cane. He greeted everyone politely and took his seat. I liked him at once, but then I had loved my grandfather.

A beggar was doing the rounds. She had a baby on her hip, a pathetic-looking creature of skin and bone who kept groping at a dried-up breast. Across the road a car stopped. On its side was written the legend Nigerian National Petroleum Corporation. A young man sat alone in the back seat. He wound down the window and called for bread. Every bread-seller in a hundred-metre radius converged on the spot. He selected what he wanted and threw the money on the ground. If I lived in the country it is such incidents that would turn me into a Marxist, whatever my reservations: such reservations as I had were a luxury.

It was dark when we reached Benin City. I was engaged in conversation all the way by a businessman: 'Import–export,' he said. He was missing the little finger on his right hand. He had lost it in the civil war. He wanted us to do some business together. What did people in England want that Nigeria could provide? I could only think of mangoes and avocado pears. He would set up a company to export; I would import: we would both make a killing. He gave me his card and insisted we get together in Lagos.

The Benin–Lagos Expressway was in poor shape. From *The Guardian* (1.8.85):

The highway was constructed about four years ago. Samuel Fadahunsi, president of the Council of Registered Engineers of Nigeria (COREN) wonders if the highway in the first place had design or specification. He says the section of the road – Ore to Benin – is in a terrible condition, because that portion of the road only had a slight cement base, suggesting the possibility of the contractors neglecting the two or three feet layer requirement.

Once we ran straight into a tree branch that had been placed in the middle of the road. We soon saw why. An articulated lorry was sprawled on its side across two lanes. It had probably swerved at high speed to avoid another vehicle and hit a pothole in the process. But we were all jumpy. The branch could have been placed there by armed robbers. This was the method they used to stop cars at night. And it was fear of armed robbers that made the police at the check-points equally jumpy. One couldn't blame them. For N75 a week they were asked to put themselves in the firing line: armed robbers, who would outnumber them three to one, wouldn't think twice about killing them. The general climate of fear nearly landed us all in trouble. Wanting to get the journey over as quickly as possible, the driver didn't at first see the policeman flagging him down with a torch. By the time he saw the torchlight he had to brake hard and pull over.

'Get down, get down,' the policeman shouted, pointing his gun at him.

'P.C., excuse me P.C.,' the elderly man said, leaning across the driver.

'Sah.'

'Please, I'm a magistrate. I know this man is in the wrong. I've warned him once before. He should have stopped immediately he saw your signal. It won't happen again, I promise you.'

The policeman relented and let us go. At a junction called Shagamu we took a short break. Long-distance lorries lined the roadside. People with makeshift stalls sold food by candlelight. I bought a cup of Bournvita. I could have had fried egg on bread: the enterprising young man whose stall I had chosen kept a wood fire burning under a pan of oil.

'Do quick, do quick,' I snapped as he waited for the water to come to the boil. Give me one year in the country and I will become a proper Nigerian. I was joined by the businessman. He said that after the war he had made his money selling foodstuffs on the roadside before he had been able to make his way to Lagos.

We reached Lagos at ten. It had been a marathon journey. In one day I had covered hundreds of kilometres; in six weeks I had covered thousands. I had gone from the dense bush forest of the south to the open savannah of the north and back again; from the extreme south-west to the extreme north-east. I was exhausted. I certainly couldn't have coped with the inside of another long-distance taxi, no matter how romantic they had seemed at first. When I got to the bungalow, Akin was watching television. He sent the maid out for beer. I had a few days to unwind before returning to England.

10

'The less we understand of what our fathers and forefathers sought, the less we understand ourselves, and thus we help with all our might to rob the individual of his roots and his guiding instincts, so that he becomes a particle in the mass . . .'
(C. G. Jung: *Memories, Dreams, Reflections*)

IN THE COURSE of that last week my depression worsened. I suppose it had something to do with the journey coming to an end; but it also had something to do with my exhaustion. Now that the journey was over I was forced to face the fact that the precise nature of my relationship to the country was as ambiguous as when I had started out. In a sense nothing had really been resolved; but in another sense I was beginning to realize that nothing could be resolved. And I didn't have the stamina to think out the implications.

It was only later, during the course of writing this book, that I began to see the ambiguity as a source of strength. On the one hand I was destined to make a journey away from my father's country, a journey begun by my grandfather with his conversion to Christianity and continued by my father with his marriage to an Englishwoman; on the other hand – and this was equally true – I was also destined to make the journey back again, to rediscover something important about myself that had been lost in that move. In other words I was tied to the country forever. I knew I would continue to return as often as I could. Perhaps my father had himself known this. His last act on earth was to leave me a small property in Lagos.

I hadn't bargained on this. After my rupture with him I had assumed I would get nothing. I had broken with him and by extension with his country. My inheritance changed everything. There is no gainsaying bricks and mortar. I went to see the property the weekend before I left. It was in an area called Suru-Lere, on the mainland, tucked away in a quiet cul-de-sac behind one of the main roads that led into the city. Because he had tied it up in a trust fund, it wouldn't come to me for another five years. That didn't diminish its reality. There it stood and it was mine. If I had doubted it before I could not doubt it now.

It would all have been much easier if I had been a different person, if I had wanted to be a lawyer or a doctor or a university lecturer. I would have fitted in better with bourgeois Lagos society, where all the talk was about money: who was making it and who wasn't. I appeared to be making it – I was here, after all – but I knew it wasn't strictly accurate. I was a writer, but not the kind of writer it seemed to me Akin would understand. I was interested in money – who isn't? – but not primarily so. Literature meant more to me than the ability to eat in expensive restaurants.

The day before I left was Independence Day. The country was officially twenty-five years old. It rained all morning. If I had been inclined to go along to the celebrations I thought better of it. I watched it on the television instead. It was a dismal affair. An endless procession of schoolchildren, soaked to the skin, paraded past the new Head of State, who was also soaked to the skin.

It cleared up at lunchtime. Akin and I went to a Chinese restaurant for a take-away. His sister was having some friends round. The meal didn't go as well as it might have. I had an argument with Akin's elder brother. I forget how we got on to the subject but I was upset by the virulence with which he attacked the Indian community in Nigeria, who number about 5,000 in Lagos alone. Unlike the Lebanese, who inter-marry and take chieftaincy titles, the Indians keep very much to themselves. They were scum, he said; if he had his way he would drive them all out tomorrow morning. I told him it was irresponsible talk but he was having none of it.

I hadn't bought as many gifts as I had wanted. On my last day Akin took time off a busy schedule and drove me around Lagos. We were looking for the Hausa traders who sold leather goods. But the War Against Indiscipline had been too successful. They had been driven off the streets. We called in at a roadside snack bar. The young woman rather too hastily opened the bottles of Coke. Akin put his hand against them in turn and then asked her why one of them was warm. She said it was because the electricity had been cut off overnight. He asked her why, in that case, the other was cold. She shrugged:

'What do you want me to do? I have already opened them.'

'Give me another cold one,' Akin said.

'What will I do with this one?'

'That's not my problem,' Akin said. They stood and watched each other. Neither was going to give in. Finally Akin turned to me: 'Oya, let's go.'

In the car he said: 'I thought she opened them fast. Some people are stupid.'

He drove me to the offices of one of the newspapers. I had arranged to meet the literary editor to discuss the possibility of sending them book reviews from England. I had met him through another schoolfriend who had once worked as a journalist on the same paper. This is the way things are done in Nigeria. Everything is dependent on personal contacts. Nigeria isn't unique in this respect. Nepotism is a feature of all societies, if only because the urge to help one's family and friends and those of the same class and background comes naturally to us all. But there must be checks. Nepotism is dangerous. It makes a society inefficient because it is hardly ever the right person who is appointed to the job.

The man hadn't arrived. I was directed to the waiting room. Half-a-dozen hopeful journalists were there ahead of me. They were all checking through grubby, hand-written manuscripts. Many of them would be here for the rest of the day trying to secure an appointment with somebody influential. Their chances weren't good, but it was all they could do. To simply leave a manuscript with the secretary would be futile. In the unlikely event that she passed it on to the editor concerned there was little chance that he would read further than the first paragraph before ditching it in the bin. The amount of patience required in Nigeria to get anything done is something that has to be experienced to be understood. I first understood when I tried to buy some stamps at the main post office. At one counter I was told there was no change; at another that he was out of stamps; and at the third I was kept waiting an inordinate amount of time when the clerk had an argument with the woman in front of me for showing him insufficient respect. Somebody ought to compute the number of working hours that are wasted in this way. I, less patient and with a plane to catch, waited only thirty minutes and left.

On my way out I was stopped by a young man. He was clutching a sheaf of papers to his chest. He asked if he could see me.

'Do you live in Nigeria or abroad?'

'Abroad, in England,' I said.

He seemed disappointed. I asked him what the problem was. He said he was looking for people to help him with a project. He was dramatizing an Achebe novel for the stage. Why he was going into a newspaper office was beyond me.

'So you're a playwright,' I said. We shook hands. I caught a taxi back to Akin's. His sister asked me if she could cook me a meal but I declined: I was already beginning to get nervous. We went to the university to pick up his wife, then drove to the airport. On the way the engine started smoking. Within minutes the inside of the car was filled with thick, black smoke. We pulled over and opened the bonnet. A loose wire was rubbing against the frame. Masking tape would fix it. There was a garage nearby. Akin called over a mechanic. He pointed out what was wrong, told him what to do and gave him N1 for his troubles. This wasn't the first time the car had broken down. A Mini in Lagos is trouble, since the undercarriage is so close to the ground. Whenever it broke down Akin would leave me with the car and catch a taxi to his local garage to pick up Alfred, his personal mechanic. Alfred was a short man with splayed feet who could take forever tightening a screw. He had an assistant. If Akin shouted at Alfred, Alfred would shout at his assistant: everybody must have someone they can shout at, if only for the sake of their dignity.

At the airport I checked in before we went for a meal. As my bag was being weighed a soldier came over.

'Who is the owner of this?' he demanded, hitting it with his baton.

'I am,' I said, trying to hide my nervousness.

'Open it.'

He rummaged around, nodded, and left.

'Why do they have to behave like that?' Shade said. We went to the restaurant. It was hot inside. Akin turned a nearby fan in our direction and switched it on. A waiter came hurrying over and promptly switched it off.

'What's the matter with you?' Akin demanded.

'Too many customers spoil it,' he said aggressively. Shade touched Akin's arm: 'Leave it, it doesn't matter.'

Akin said to the waiter: 'You are very stupid.' The waiter departed in a huff. We were kept waiting forty minutes before our order was taken. By that time I had lost what little appetite I had.

The last time I left the country I had to bribe the immigration official before he would stamp my passport. This was because my visa was out of date by twenty-four hours. It hadn't been my fault: it had been the fault of the immigration officer on my way in. I had started arguing but quickly gave up. It hadn't taken me long to realize that they were working a system. In Nigeria you make the most of what you've got.

This time it was different. The man ahead of me, whose visa was out of date, had put a N5 note between the pages of his passport. The official let the money drop on the desk and gazed at it for a moment. Then he looked up at the man and said, quietly but firmly, 'Please take your money.'

I had been foolish to have got so worked up.

I had flown in with Sierra Leone Airlines and I flew out with them. My travel agent in Tunbridge Wells had only been able to exchange my Egypt Air ticket with them by booking a return flight. It was even the same Boeing 707. I know because I had the same seat and they still hadn't fixed the overhead light. The pilot was the same Jordanian and we were looked after by the same cabin crew.

At Freetown, where we had to wait five hours, the man from whom I had bought the shirt with my excess naira was still there. He recognized me. He said that he wished he hadn't agreed to sell it to me because he hadn't been able to change the money. It was useless to him. To mollify him I bought a few beads for my wife with some of the sterling I had on me.

We fell to talking. He told me that he had been a sailor when he was younger. He had travelled all over the world. He liked what he had seen of Europe, especially Amsterdam and London. He couldn't say what Cape Town was like because they weren't allowed off the ship, although women were allowed to come aboard. He hadn't been to Russia but he knew he wouldn't like it. In fact he hated the Russians. This is because they had killed his best friend who was a student there a few years ago. The authorities had shot him and dumped his body in a river because they thought he was an American spy. It had taken his friend's family three months to find out that he was dead. At first they couldn't understand why their letters kept coming back. Eventually they found out but it took weeks to get the body back.

This time we didn't call in at Las Palmas, but we did stop over in Paris. It was early morning. The colours here were sombre after the dazzling African light. An hour later we touched down in London. Efficiency was the order of the day. The officials were polite and everything worked. One didn't need a military escort to ease one's passage through the various formalities.